A Message From Overseas

ANTHONY W. LoCASCIO

DEDICATION

To Grandma and Grandpa: your stories never stopped captivating me.
~ Anthony

This book is dedicated to my four children and their wonderful spouses.
You do so much to take care of me, and I hope you enjoy my story.
~ Grandma Eve

CONTENTS

Acknowledgments i

Chapter 1 1

Chapter 2 9

Chapter 3 16

Chapter 4 22

Chapter 5 27

Chapter 6 33

Chapter 7 39

Chapter 8 45

Chapter 9 53

Chapter 10 59

Chapter 11 66

Letter from Eva 74

Afterword 76

Endnotes/Credits 78

About the Author 79

ACKNOWLEDGMENTS

My heartfelt thanks go out to Grandma, for spending all those hours with me while I feverishly typed every word, and to my wife, Marina, for her support, keeping me motivated throughout the writing process.

CHAPTER 1

"YOU CANNOT SWIM FOR NEW HORIZONS UNTIL YOU HAVE
COURAGE TO LOSE SIGHT OF THE SHORE."
— WILLIAM FAULKNER

Gus and Antonia are young—kids by today's standards—when they meet, fall in love, and start their family. Neither of them has ventured much outside their Italian province of Frosinone by the time the first baby arrives. But together they grow and work and share their dreams.

Born in 1897, Gustavo was adopted from a local orphanage. Gustavo's adoptive parents, the Violantis, raised him on their farm in Giuliano di Roma. Giuliano di Roma rests in Frosinone, only a dozen or so miles from its namesake capital city, where Gustavo was found as a child. As is customary, Gustavo was not bestowed his adoptive family's name, but instead kept his bastard surname, Ovarsi. However, Gus, as he is affectionately known by those closest to him, grows up knowing very little about his lineage, his birth family, or their profession. He's not even positive he has the proper names. Rumors swirl that Gustavo is actually of Swiss descent, due to his light features and apparent confusion about how he ended up in Frosinone... but all Gustavo will ever know is how to be a Violanti.

Maria Antonia Gabrielli is a pretty Giuliano girl two years younger than Gustavo. Due to the sheer number of women named "Maria" throughout Italy, Frosinone being no exception, friends and family call her Antonia.

She, like all the other middle-class girls, learned to sew and cook in her youth.

They are a happy family, but are anxious for a better life. The couple live during a tumultuous time: Italy is being rocked by worker strikes and the people have embraced fascism to quell the upheaval. Antonia and Gustavo look to other horizons, ones filled with opportunity and stability rather than the fears and anxieties rooted in the changing landscape around them.

Antonia also struggles with tragedy in Italy, albeit a tragedy that is not uncommon for the times. During the 1920s, she births three daughters: Mimi, Minna, and Iona. The first two pass away of rhesus disease before their first birthdays, Mimi at nine months and Minna at eleven months. Antonia deals with all this heartache without the support of her husband. The couple had become enamored by the promise of an avenue to prosperity, so Gustavo left their home at twenty-three, scouting the path ahead to America. For years, beginning in 1921, he travels back and forth in order to prepare to move the family. He works as a farmer, returning to Italy when he is able: only two or three times in eight years. The majority of his time is spent in America, planning for the day his family can join him.

Antonia is not bitter about her husband's chronic absence, however. She is not jealous, and she is not resentful. She understands that this sacrifice of her husband's time and attention may provide something much greater: the safety and prosperity of the family. She is grateful for having married a strong and steadfast man with the determination to make a successful emigration to the United States possible. She is optimistic in the face of a daunting reality: that The Great Depression has made life as different in America as in Giuliano. She believes that all this sacrifice will lead to lifelong happiness for herself and her children. (And she is partly right—but she does not fully anticipate the enormous hardship that lies ahead.)

When the time is right, Gustavo keeps his promise to prepare the way for his beloved Antonia, so that they may start their new lives as Americans.

He returns from America with the exciting news that he will not be departing again without his wife and child. Antonia has the pleasure of announcing that there may be more than one child joining their trip. Gus is a swirl of emotions. He is ecstatic to hear that his wife is pregnant, but also terrified at the thought of imposing the horrors of the oceanic voyage on a newborn. All plans to reach America with his family are expedited as much as possible.

Records show that the ship that the Ovarsi family arrived on originally launched in 1927. Its colorful history includes being seized by Brazil in 1941 and later becoming a US troop transport in WWII, before returning to Italian services in 1949. The ship was renamed twice: first to the *Monticello* in 1941; and later to the *Conte Grande* in 1947.[1] The original name during the time of the Ovarsis' voyage has not been confirmed.

It is 1929 when the visibly-pregnant Antonia, Iona (her last remaining daughter of three), and Gustavo depart for the US on the *Vittorio Emmanuel III*. The 624-foot ship boasts two massive funnels, billowing steam that will trace its path through the Atlantic air for miles. Iona is a petite girl with deep brown hair and hazel eyes. She is full of energy, usually prancing around and giggling, but is also very mature and can be relied upon by Antonia to behave without much trouble. But the Port of Naples seems recklessly disorganized.

Masses of people swarm the docks. Could Ellis Island be any worse? By all accounts, it feels like a miracle to Antonia that she even made it through the ninety-mile trek from Giuliano to Naples, as well as through the cursory medical exam to board the ship. She is gripped by sudden apprehension when she considers the ten airless days it will take to reach America.

In June of 1929, Antonia delivers her newborn below deck, amid many hundreds of fellow travelers who watch in weary silence. The baby girl seems healthy, bawling with a pair of powerful lungs. Her wails, however, are no match for the deafening hum of the engines nearby. Iona gazes on from a cluttered bunk, tears running down her face, while her father comforts her. She rolls in her hand a wrinkled playing card that she found soon after leaving Italy. The ship left a few weeks ago, but the trials of the voyage make it feel as if months have passed. Dozens of passengers have already passed away, and a few unclaimed corpses crammed are under the filth, among the living. The baby, heedless to this, cries herself out before settling with contentment at her mother's breast.

The clunky ship finally lumbers into the dark waters surrounding the New York islands. The Statue of Liberty waves warmly to all those aboard who are lucky enough to either be above deck or near a porthole window. The Ovarsis are in steerage and have seen nothing--smelled nothing--but rot and sick for weeks. Antonia and Gus worry over how the Americans will react to their baby's unintentional trespass. More pressingly, the young mother is determined to provide American citizenship for the newborn. Hushed exaggerations trickle through the corridors about the awe-inspiring size of "Miss Liberty", tales of speechless wonder about the goddess who just welcomed them, made with the understanding that her grandeur represents the power of the country that is to be their home.

Just beyond the statue, about a half-mile to the northwest, is Ellis Island. After the ship docks in Manhattan, while cabin passengers are released to the freedom of New York, steerage passengers pour across the pier to a waiting area. Each wears a name tag with their manifest number written in large figures. The immigrants are assembled into groups of about thirty and are packed on the top decks of barges while their baggage is piled below. Although they are finally above board and riding in the open air, the dense crowd of putrid steerage passengers keeps the atmosphere close and suffocating. Gus lifts Iona up on his shoulders so she may rise above it and fill her lungs with the fresh sea air. Antonia hides the new baby under her dress, determined to conceal her until they can claim the birth on American soil.

Upon disembarkation, the shrill shouts of a dozen different languages assault their ears. Interpreters are the first Americans the migrants meet. The interpreters lead groups from the barges and into Ellis Island through the main doorway and then up a steep stairway to the Registry Room, nicknamed the Great Hall. Although they do not realize it, the immigrants are already participating in their first test. A medical doctor stands at the top of the stairs watching for signs of lameness, indications of heart conditions, or empty "bewildered" gazes that might be symptomatic of a mental condition. Any such indication is enough to direct the weary traveler back whence they came.[2]

The Great Hall is exactly that, an expansive room with sky-high vaulted ceilings and enormous arching windows. In defiance of its size, the lines are long, and the hall is stuffed full with immigrants. As each immigrant files in, the doctors, accompanied by interpreters, examine the immigrant's face, hair, neck, and hands. In order to get through the mobs of delirious travelers, the doctors have a mere six seconds to make an assessment before using a white piece of chalk to scrawl a large letter indicating whether or not that entrant must be detained for further medical inspection. [2]

If immigrants have any one of many enumerated diseases, or are simply determined to be too ill, they are promptly prepared for deportation. Sickly teenagers are separated from their families and turned back to their home countries. Sobbing parents compose themselves and decide who will accompany younger children home, as they cannot be removed without a guardian to oversee their return voyage. [2]

With children of all ages being wrangled by parents and older siblings, it is impossible to keep from nudging and bumping others in line. Cumbersome suitcases and bundles of warm clothes seem to wiggle free from people's arms. Ellis Island is crowded and stifling, but the energy is largely positive. The long, arduous journey from Europe, across the Atlantic Ocean, and into America is nearing its end for the passengers of the *Vittorio*

Emmanuel III.

"NEXT!" the primary line inspector yells toward the rows of befuddled immigrants.

This is the final test. The young man ahead of Antonia moves on after speaking with the grumpy uniform perched on his tall stool. Gustavo takes Antonia's hand. The exhausted interpreters sling through variations of greetings to quickly ascertain the best dialect for communication.

"Are you next?! Please step forward!" The grumpy man gestures irritably at Antonia and Iona.

"We must be next," Antonia says to Iona in their native Italian, but Iona doesn't respond. Her eyes are darting nervously as she looks up and around at all the weary travelers heavily garbed in layers of clothing and coats.

Gustavo is stopped in line behind his wife by immigration officers, who gesture for him to wait his turn. The head of the family and the only one to have experienced the ordeal of entering America is barred from helping his wife and child. Antonia and Iona gather up all of their belongings, careful not to startle or hurt the little infant under Antonia's dress, and approach the agent without Gustavo to help.

"Name?" The inspector has an important job, and—if he is expected to review each and every body that steps off these barges each day—only a few precious minutes to spend on each immigrant brought before him.

"Ovarsi."

"Yes, I know you are from overseas…" Frustrated from the long day, the inspector slows down his speech and raises his voice. "But what's your NAME?"

Confused, Antonia says again, "Ovarsi. Ovarsi." She darts her head around, looking for Gustavo.

The inspector glances desperately at his watch. 2:16. Just over thirty seconds since the last time he checked, and they've only just begun.

The inspector swipes the bridge of his greasy nose and runs his fingers over his mustachioed lip. He decides to pick up his paperwork and show it to Antonia, speaking in rough and brutish Italian. "What is your *NO-ME?*"

The interpreter, confused by the miscommunication, clams up.

"Mi chiamo, *O-var-si*!" Antonia mimics the officer's inflection and jabs at the paper with her finger.

Wasn't the Registry enough? she thinks to herself.

Fully understanding now, the officer sheepishly begins writing down Antonia's information. He spells the name 'Ovarzi' on the immigration paperwork. Antonia realizes the error, but also knows that she is dealing with authorities on borrowed time: the hidden baby is waking up and is due for a feeding. If Antonia and Iona don't get out of immigration soon, they may all be in danger.

Soon Antonia and Iona have completed the checkpoints, but they are still on the premises. The baby starts kicking hard and grabbing at Antonia's clothes. The mother-and-daughter duo double their pace among the excited gang headed out of the processing. Security notices them, but turns away to eye up some rowdy men.

The baby is beginning to cry, and Antonia needs to nurse her. Antonia stifles the baby's sobs as she pushes through the final turnstiles. She kicks her head back toward the sky before filling her lungs with a deep breath of crisp, salty air. She holds back the desire to weep with relief.

Later, children in tow, Antonia and her husband arrive on the streets of Hoboken, New Jersey. They embrace each other.

"Dammi la mia bambina," Gustavo gently commands. His eyes well with a father's love as he gazes at his newborn and bends down to hug Iona. Another baby girl—another reminder of the ones he has lost—but nonetheless a joyous gift from God.

They are in America now. She has taken them in like the proverbial innkeeper during a storm and provided only that which they need to heal, rest, and get moving again. Gustavo and Antonia will always remember the sprightly lives their union lost, but it has not made them bitter. They have not been made callous to the world or driven to renounce their faith. Instead, tragedy has hardened their resolve, and they have embraced their religion in search of comfort. In another dedication to God for his many blessings, such as safe passage from Italy and the delivery of a healthy child, Gus and Antonia bestow the newborn with the biblical name of Eva. The name means "life." The doting parents are determined to protect Eva's own life from the plague that took Mimi's and Minna's. They will do everything they can to ensure she has a good future, and that their sacrifices were not made in vain.

What opportunities will America hold for Gustavo and Antonia? It is not important to them. What opportunities does it hold for their children? Such a question has no answer. *Anything*, Gustavo believes: anything is possible now. They are all equals here. Gustavo will find that he is not correct in all of his assumptions, but in this moment the anxiety of future struggles, both anticipated and unforeseen, is dormant. The exhausted family sets off for their first home of many to come in the next few years.

Gustavo leads his long-awaited guests to the relatively lush apartment of Uncle Joseph, known lovingly as Zio Peppino. Zio Peppino, his wife, Zia Maria, and Cugino Filippo are Antonia's relatives. Gustavo has been staying with them on occasion in their Hoboken apartment, located at the intersection of 4th Street and Garden Street, a stone's throw away from the main avenue. The tenement building sits across from the David E. Rue Junior High School, an all-boys school which will groom the minds of Frank Sinatra and other Jersey boys both famous and infamous. Zio Peppino's apartment boasts three bedrooms, a large kitchen, a living room, and a separate room outfitted specifically for vinifying wine. They are kind people who take it as a personal pleasure to show the new arrivals hospitality. Zio Peppino insists that Gustavo move his family into the available apartment one story below. It's possible—anything is possible. Gustavo knows he cannot afford the luxury of limiting his options yet. He must be open to any move or any job, so long as it serves to benefit the family. They dine together that night, saying a prayer and breaking bread before a meal of pasta and pork. Although anxiety about the future is beginning to affect Gustavo and Antonia, the mood at dinner remains jubilant. The family is together again.

CHAPTER 2

"A BEND IN THE ROAD IS NOT THE END OF THE ROAD... UNLESS YOU FAIL TO MAKE THE TURN."
— HELEN KELLER

All four Ovarsis sleep together on the floor of Zio Peppino's living room each night for a month. Eva, the strong and healthy baby girl, must still be christened as an American, for, as of now, she is devoid of all allegiances. Gustavo and Antonia bring Eva to Saint Mary's Hospital, where she is "officially" born: she is provided a birth certificate and registered as a "natural-born citizen" at the Hoboken Municipal Building. What will life have in store for the little girl who was birthed aboard a transatlantic voyage and smuggled into the world's foremost emerging superpower? It is October 22, and Eva finally has the anniversary she will celebrate as her birthday for the rest of her life.

Now, la famiglia Ovarsi is equally as American as they are Italian. Gustavo already achieved his United States citizenship prior to fetching Antonia and Iona. He, along with Eva, makes up two of four members of the family to be true Americans.

Gustavo came to the States to work for a better life. He sought paychecks wherever he could get them. He was born to pursue the American dream, and he had the tools for success, as a physically and mentally tough person. These attributes are nothing short of necessary when trying to succeed as a man in his position. Soon after Eva's Hoboken "birth," Gustavo leads his family off of Zio Peppino's floor and into Tunkhannock, Pennsylvania. For a year, Gustavo takes on various manual labor stints. Then the Ovarsi patriarch gets a job in Newark, New Jersey, working as a yardman for Lackawanna Railroad Company. Newark's Pennsylvania Train Station is still a couple years from completion. Gus spends his days filling the refrigerator cars with ice and hammering new track into the burgeoning New Jersey landscape.

Life in Newark, however, isn't all work. The couple of years spent there bring a few more additions to the family. Just as Eva was delivered by a midwife while on the *Vittorio Emmanuel III*, Antonia enlists the help of midwives while giving birth to her next two children. Bambini Iolanda, who will eventually prefer to be called Linda, and Mario are born in quick succession in 1932 and 1933.

Employment on the railroad eventually tugs the Ovarsis back to where they started their American tale: Hoboken. Antonia finds employment with Lackawanna too, serving as a bathroom matron in the Lackawanna Station that sits waterfront at the southernmost point of town. The apartment below Zio Peppino is still available, and what better place for an immigrant family to be than close to relatives? Little Eva is now five years old, and although she will see many more changes to her address, the Ovarsi family will call Hoboken home for the rest of their lives.

Hoboken is a bustling urban city. It sits wedged between the Hudson River to the east and the sheer cliff face of the Palisades to the west. The northern and southern ends of this single square-mile city are squeezed in by minor waterways. With nowhere to go, Hoboken stares longingly at the growing New York City skyline. Like a younger brother, Hoboken's micro-culture mimics that of the Big Apple. Segregated ethnic neighborhoods made up of Italians, Irishmen, and Germans fill the cityscape a few blocks at a time.

Living within the proper circles means you are part of a community. More than just being neighbors, sharing a common heritage bestows a network of requited support. That network is invaluable to those who battle with the realities of poverty. The Ovarsi family is not unique in its ever-increasing size. Failing to afford a hospital visit during labor is also a common occurrence here. The Ovarsi household is a three-room, shotgun-style apartment, where each room runs into the next without doors or hallways. Each floor holds two apartments that share a communal bathroom. The bathrooms are sparse, offering no tubs, no showers, and no hot water. Sponge baths are taken in water basins filled with water straight off the coal-burning stove. That is all Gustavo can afford. That is all most of the blue-collar Hoboken residents can afford. This arrangement forces neighbors to interact, for better or for worse. The Ovarsis consider themselves lucky. They get along very well with their neighbors, the Cinsolis. Mrs. Helen Cinsoli, a woman of Irish descent who married into her Italian surname, serves as Antonia's encyclopedia for all things "*Medigan.*"

While living and cavorting in the Italian district, it is easy for little Eva to forget there are non-Italians in town. However, the storefronts along Washington Street and the adjacent side streets display the city's diverse populace. It is apparent to Eva who can be counted on to own what. The Jews own small professional businesses, the Italians own restaurants, and the Irish and the Germans own mostly bars and taverns.

It is often necessary to leave the comforts of one's neighborhood. For the Italian children, such as Eva, this is the case every time they walk to school. In 1934, Eva is entering kindergarten, and the Irish and the Italians are feuding. Oblivious to this, she is only excited for her first day of school. Iona has been held back more than a year due to not knowing English, and she is beginning second grade. None of the Ovarsis speak English fluently. In fact, they have only picked up enough tortured English to speak with necessary vendors, cashiers, and trusted friends.

Eva's route to elementary school takes her through the Irish neighborhood. No one is spared the indignities served between the two nationalities, regardless of age or gender. Iona accompanies Eva every morning on her trek to homeroom. Their path traverses 1st Street, one block from P.S. No. 9 Elementary School, which is located at 2nd and Monroe. Shrill voices can be heard as the neighborhood takes notice of the trespassers' arrival. There always seems to be time for picking fights. Strong and resolute, eight-year-old Iona provides support and guidance to her scared sibling. She tells Eva to ignore the heckling schoolchildren.

"Here come the 'Guineas'!" The young women lead the jeers—true cheerleaders. "WOPs!"

Eva has never heard these words before, but they sting as intended. Virulent hate speech pours forth, and although she has no idea what it all means, she is stunned by its viciousness. The abuse doesn't stop at slinging epithets. Schoolbooks prove to be humble and effective bludgeons. Iona buries her anguish and attempts to convince Eva that the goons are just playing rough as she pulls her little sis to school. They turn the corner and dive into their respective homerooms.

Eva's first day does not improve greatly from her morning commute. Her foreign-born ears cannot understand the English-speaking teachers, and maintaining attention on the day's lesson is impossible for the creative young mind. Her head swims with daydreams and day terrors. Her slog through the 7 a.m. onslaught haunts her. Once the concluding school bell blares, Eva and Iona sprint home to safety.

As soon as the children enter their apartment, the steely resolve they displayed throughout the day melts away. They describe every horrid detail of the morning's trial to their mother.

"They hit us and called us 'Guineas!'"

Antonia does not understand these slurs that the hooligans are calling her daughters. Not daring to cross the threshold, Eva and Iona watch as their mother leaps the three feet to the Cinsolis's front door. Helen is quick to answer.

"Che e' 'Guinea?'" Antonia quizzes Helen brusquely.

Helen is stupefied. She has no idea what it means either, but she can tell how upset the family is. She recruits the aid of her husband, Tony.

Exhausted from a long day of work, he explains, "They're calling you dirty and low-class."

Antonia roars. This is their home, and this is unacceptable. Antonia is determined that the ambush will never happen again... at least not unpunished.

The next morning, Helen and Antonia secretly tail the girls on their way to school. The Irish children wait for the prey to present itself. As soon as Helen and Antonia hear the assault, Antonia springs unrestrained. The mother of four plunges headlong into the melee. She swings with purpose, and her attacks catch the intended targets. The opponents range in age, the oldest being preteens. She smacks them all repeatedly with her pocketbook, and the kids scatter, shrieking like bruised and beaten hyenas. The day has been won, in defense of the Italian ragazze. Antonia anticipates fallout from her actions, but she is not overly concerned. After all, if this were Italy, one could expect the entire neighborhood to be involved in the levying of just deserts.

When the Irish parents find out the cause of their children's crusty noses and ragged locks, they haul them over to Antonia's four-story and force the pugnacious agitators to apologize. The children vow never to do it again. It is a turning point for the attendees of Public School Number 9. Relationships improve over the following months. Friendships form, and the Ovarsi girls find English tutors in their old adversaries. A few freckle-faced redheads can later be observed speaking Italian as well.

Once Eva and Iona adjust to public school, time begins passing quickly and the Ovarsi family is unable to settle at any one address for very long. With each new Hoboken apartment, a new family member seems sure to follow. In 1934, the second son, Gus Jr., is born at a home found on 1st Street near Monroe. Rosemary, Eva's youngest and final sibling, is born while living at 73 Jefferson Street in 1937.

The locations may be named after different presidents, but the circumstances of each birth are nearly identical. Nativity is a community event. Eva and the rest of the children in the apartment building wait in the hall for the midwife to deliver the newborns. During Rosemary's delivery, every woman from the building is seemingly in the Ovarsi apartment attending to Antonia. Privacy is scant, as the kids of the neighborhood, strewn about the hall and dangling off steps, can hear Antonia's struggle. Eva's friend Sally Briguglio, a short boy with dirty hands who will later be known as Sally Bugs, leans over to reassure her that everything will be alright.

As the years have passed, the area has continued to serve as a nursery for clashes between cultures, especially between the "new" immigrants and the "old."[3] Although everyone is proud to be American, assimilation does not occur overnight. The Ovarsis are no different from any other immigrant parents. They expect their children to grow up embracing their roots.

Around the time of Rosemary's birth, Gustavo signs all the children up for weekend sessions at a co-ed Italian school, located on 1st Street and Garden Street. The school does not shy away from educating the pupils on the greatness of Italy and, especially, the greatness of its leader, Benito Mussolini. The parents of the attendees are well aware of and quietly support the fascist teachings. The children recite fascist anthems and wear the fascist uniforms: black skirts or pants, black neckties, and white, long-sleeved, collared shirts. Some minor deviations from the uniform are permitted. There is one detail that is indisputably required, however. Each student must don a black sash around their upper-left arm. It is an armband that reads "ITALIA" in large block lettering.

The children wear this mark of their ancestral home with great pride.

Eva (*left*) on the day of her Confirmation, with her godmother

CHAPTER 3

"RISK COMES FROM NOT KNOWING WHAT YOU ARE DOING."
— WARREN BUFFETT

During her school years, Eva is always outside playing, at least when she's not singing, dancing, or studying. It is the same for every Hoboken child. There really isn't much choice, because no one has the space to play inside.

There aren't many toys around the neighborhood. The humble rubber ball is the most important prize young Hobokenites have. The owner of chalk is the king of the block. Spare (or stolen) rope from a laundry line is more valuable than gold. These trinkets and baubles are priceless to the neighborhood children, who are genuinely happy. They don't need anything more.

Beyond simple games such as hide-and-seek, kick-the-can, and telephone, children exercise ingenuity in an effort to elude boredom. Board games such as *Monopoly* are unnecessary on the streets. The neighborhood kids draw a large square with a piece of chalk and print the word "WAR" in the middle. Play pieces are bottle caps, stuffed and weighted with orange peels. Smaller boxes are drawn inside the chalk play area. Each box is named for a different country, the most common being Germany, Italy, Japan, Britain, France, Russia, China, and America. The caps are pinched between the thumb and forefinger and tossed into each country's box. Each one that lands within the country's bounds is a successful "hit." The caps fill boxes until the country is sacked. WAR keeps the kids busy for hours.

A second game, one that causes its fair share of rope burns, is named Lerio. A large circle is drawn in chalk, and the children arrange themselves around it. The player in the middle has a rope to swing while kids run around the circle. If the rope finds a target and wraps around a kid's leg, then that player is 'out.' The number of children along the ring determines how many laps the contestants have to run around the ring in order to be safe from being out. The last remaining contender is deemed the winner, and takes stage in the center of the ring.

Points, a third game, is the union of Jacks and Skee-ball. A high stoop provides the ideal arena for the game. Each step is given a point value. The bottom step is worth ten points, the second is worth twenty, and so on. In turn, each player throws a ball at the edge of the steps. If the throwing player catches the ball after only hitting the step, then that player earns the points that are allocated to that step.

These three games provide many hours of entertainment and years of wonderful memories for an entire generation of children. Of course, there are times when it gets boring between street games. Perhaps the last ball has been stolen by the neighborhood dog, or the chalk has ground into an unusable nub. Something has to be done to pass the afternoon. When Eva and her friends are feeling more entrepreneurial, they walk along the street to find discarded cigarette packs. The insides of the containers are lined with silver paper, which opens up a lot of opportunities.

One day, a man with a pushcart tells the girls that if they make a silver ball weighing one pound from the cigarette linings, he will give the kids five cents! Five cents is a very attractive incentive, enough to buy a loaf of bread or five pounds of potatoes. However, being children of about ten years old, Eva and her friends are thinking about the bounty they could earn at Houten's Chocolate Shop. Coated pretzels, small hard candies, and other chocolate goodies are sold by the fistful. Small chocolate candies with a racially-charged nickname can be purchased at ten for a penny.

Riding their expectant sugar highs, Eva and the girls find other disposed items to rummage for as well as the silver paper. They begin collecting and recycling glass bottles. The deposit for each bottle varies, often by color. Some earn a penny. Others are worth two. Plastic bottles are unheard of and will not be seen for about a decade. The girls collect the glass bottles in red wagons and bring them to stores that will provide the deposit. The girls successfully earn play money throughout the summer to pay for goodies.

To pass the time on summer afternoons when it is too hot to be sprinting across charged asphalt or rummaging through stinking trash, the children find excitement in watching blimps and airplanes pass in, out, and around New York. And with their eyes on the skies in the late 1930s, the neighborhood youth notice increasing blimp traffic. Airplanes are not yet commercially available for international travel. For this reason, they are a rare sight, so rare that the kids keep record by making chalk marks for each sighting on the side of the brick homes. Learning well from the role models of the day, such as Sonny Franzese and his boys, they start gambling on the exact number of planes that will pass overhead.

Menacing storm clouds aren't even enough for the neighborhood parents to bring their children inside for the day.

On one particular May afternoon in 1937, Eva and her friends savor the cool breeze, but cannot stand the thought of kicking a can. While one pint-sized shark opts to gamble on two aircraft sightings over his competition's one, Eva and her friends notice that a familiar, low-flying blimp has made a second appearance over the Hudson River. Besides prompting an argument over whether the blimp counts as one or two sightings, the flight path also startles Gustavo.

"Antonia!" Gustavo's voice bellows from the backyard of their walk-up where he is feeding chickens.

There's a clash of windows being thrown open and faces poking out to stare upward at the eerily slow-moving blimp. The entire city strains their necks toward the lighter-than-air ship slowly lumbering by. Gustavo, less mesmerized and more frantic, thinks a bombing is imminent and screams for Antonia to get the kids to safety, inside and under the beds. His intensity seems to electrify the rest of his neighbors, his excitement arcing from one to another. The Ovarsis don't own a television, so Antonia tunes the radio to the Italian station. It is of no benefit. The delayed landing of the *Hindenburg* is apparently not newsworthy.

They learn later that day that the luxury transcontinental airship crashed while setting down at Lakehurst Naval Air Station in New Jersey. Very few of the Hoboken residents know where Lakehurst, New Jersey is, but the story of the huge craft being devoured in flames in a mere half-minute circulates throughout the town for weeks. No one survived the inferno that resulted from the German ship being coated in rocket fuel prior to flying amidst a lightning storm. Although the tragedy has nothing to do with military aggression, it will be later argued by living room lectors and parlor pontificators that the arrogance exhibited by the Germans in the late 1930s was an overlooked warning of the war that will consume the globe in a few years' time.

Although incomes are still generally low among its citizens, Hoboken is constantly expanding and improving. It is reaping the financial benefits of tremendous immigration, as well as from commercial shipping routes that dock at Hoboken's Hudson River port. Profits are spent to improve life for the citizens, and in the 1940s, Hoboken builds a recreation center. The center offers afterschool and weekend care, where children of all ages can play games and sports, attend dances, or take various lessons, all provided at no cost.

Eva loves learning all of the new games—real games of which the kids never knew. Hoboken children are now experiencing bingo, chess, and, Eva's favorite, checkers. Since a crushed can was the most advanced plaything most children had south of 12th Street, the new games are stunning, visually-spectacular in their candy-colorful packaging. Teenaged boys monopolize the basketball courts, while their young admirers swoon from the sidelines. There is a room for learning to sew buttons and arrange flowers. There is a horse range, a device used to make rugs and other woven projects. Teen dances are held in the gymnasium.

Music is also a strongly supported service at the center. A music teacher wheels in an upright piano and gives voice lessons for free each week. This is where Eva meets her best childhood friend, Adelaide. Eva adores "Adey" and envies her wonderful singing voice. They sing together and teach each other to dance. Adey sings Eva's praises, exclaiming over her beautiful face and insisting Eva should model. This is the first time Eva ever thinks about modelling.

Eva is an average student, energetic and with tremendous creativity. She survives P.S. No. 9 and moves on to middle school: seventh, eighth, and ninth grades. The middle school is an all-girls junior high school, named after Joseph F. Brandt and located at 9th Street and Garden Street. Eva is quickly bestowed a new nickname. Her friends call her "Rookie," because she's always hanging around big sis Iona and her older group of friends. The name sticks.

On a mild day for December in 1941, Rookie, the starlet performer, could not be more thrilled. The Girl Scout Forum has arranged a show in

Hoboken to showcase young talents throughout the many young women's organizations. Loudspeakers are set up on the streets, so that the entire community can appreciate the sounds of children singing. The German school attendees have already completed their set and it is time for the girls of the Italian school to take center stage. Eva, Adey, and their giggling girlfriends can barely contain their excitement backstage. They are eagerly waiting for their cue when the evening's emcee introduces their troupe. After the girls flitter to center stage and take their places, no time is wasted before the upright piano chimes its first notes, and they begin belting the prepared set. This performance is designed to showcase the progress made while at school. For this reason, the students of Eva's Italian school are not just singing any pretty tune. They are singing songs in support of the Old Country, songs in support of the Italian people and their interests…

They are gleefully performing fascist anthems.

The United States' participation in The War was thrust upon the nation with the Japanese bombing of Pearl Harbor only a day prior. News of this world event is, characteristic of the time, slow to find its way into the homes of the non-English inhabitants of the East Coast. But not everyone in Hoboken is so ignorant about the Day of Infamy.

Eva and her friends have not finished their third song when the double doors of the auditorium burst open. The rattling of rusty locks, the flood of afternoon sunlight, and the booming voices of uniformed men tear through the building. The imperfect pitch of children singing immediately turns into a cacophony of shrill screams, which are answered just as quickly by the parents in the audience. The FBI has showed up to arrest the fascist supporters, and they do so with gusto.

Eva sprints to a window backstage. She and her friend, a fellow Italian vocalist named Stella, flee out the window and down the alley. As they run, they claw at their uniforms, ripping them off their bodies piecemeal. The armbands are plunged into garbage cans, and their shirts are tossed into the sewer. By the time Eva arrives home she has nearly stripped down to her slip. The sirens from police vehicles blare in the streets, and she believes the authorities will move from house to house, sending everyone to jail.

Iona is home when Eva arrives, and she understands Eva through her panicked sobbing. She instructs Eva to take the rest of her clothes off and burn them in the coal oven. Gustavo makes it home from the recital, but not Antonia. Antonia was arrested while watching Eva from her seat in the forum. Eva is rattled, visibly shaken and quivering. She had never imagined police would round their own countrymen up like animals. Even dog-catchers show more restraint. The family cannot work out how to help Antonia… so they wait.

The enthusiasm the FBI displayed while handcuffing suspected fascists and Nazi sympathizers leads the Italians and Germans of Hoboken to fear the worst. However, Antonia and most of the other detainees are not arrested, but instead are required to register at US Citizenship and Immigration Services. Eva accompanies her mother and father into New York City to USCIS while Iona watches the younger siblings. They tell the Office that Eva was born in the US to Gustavo, who is a citizen.

Antonia cannot speak English and cannot pass the citizenship test because they require a recitation of the Preamble to the Constitution. It is a hurdle she simply cannot seem to overcome and Antonia agrees with the process. In the eyes of her family, she is the greatest American, regardless of any official paper saying so. Even though she holds pride for her birth country, Antonia subscribes wholeheartedly to the American way. Her allegiances are squarely with America and its interests, and she expresses her intention to never return to Italy. So, although still not a citizen, Antonia is permitted to stay with her husband and children.

The day is very stressful. Eva finds solace for a few moments as her imagination carries her far away, watching the boats in the East River silently push through the murky winter water.

CHAPTER 4

"RISK ANYTHING! CARE NO MORE FOR THE OPINION OF
OTHERS... DO THE HARDEST THING ON EARTH FOR YOU.
ACT FOR YOURSELF."
— KATHERINE MANSFIELD,
JOURNAL ENTRY 14 OCT. 22

The War makes life more difficult for just about everyone. The lives of every Hobokenite are affected by the chilling effect of global conflict. Every rationed good and waived pay raise serves to remind the mainland residents that democracy around the world is being fought for on their behalf. Eva and Iona work hard to get by, and every cent collected or earned by the girls is donated back to the familial coffers. The play-filled days of childhood are sacrificed almost entirely by the young teens so that they might contribute to the betterment of the family.

Since the sisters are now young women, they are also expected to take on their share of the kitchen and household duties. This frees up Antonia to work a job. Eva's least favorite chore is one that demands daily attention: scrubbing the pots and pans. She also dislikes having to make a butter substitute similar to margarine. To Eva, the butter is off-putting, and churning it herself forces her to face the harsh, unappetizing realities of this unnatural fat-mash. The butter is made by hand, with a yellow pill smashed and folded into a pound of lard. Eva admits that it tastes all right, but, for her, ignorance would have provided a blissful reprieve.

During WWII in Hoboken, there are "blackouts." The towns along the water are instructed to turn off their lights, so that the coastal towns cannot be seen at night, for they fear an attack could surprise them as it did Pearl Harbor. Castle Point is the highest point in Hoboken, overlooking the Hudson River one hundred feet below. It serves as the location of Stevens Institute of Technology, a small university paying homage to the former landowner and resident, John Stevens. Castle Point's name is a corruption of "Castille Point," due to its supposed resemblance to the Castilian coast in Spain. Once a necessary light-post for sailing ships, now even Castle Point spends nights snuffed out for the protection of the port city's residents. During the day, the fort houses a school for naval officers and an intake facility for returning soldiers, the latter of whom are examined for symptoms of shell shock (or post-traumatic stress disorder, as it is now called).

Iona works an eight-hour day at Castle Point as a secretary for the officers. At 4:30 p.m., she checks out and makes her way down to the waterside to work at Todd's Shipyard until nine at night. The shipyard fixes warships for the US and British navies. Eva believes the government modeled Rosie the Riveter after her big sister. She wells with pride thinking about it. But Iona does not have an ego about her diligence, regardless of what Eva says. She is only doing what needs to be done, and she is one of thousands of women taking a small part in supporting the war effort while bringing what money they can to the household.

It is not a time for anyone to sit idle if they are capable of working. Eva and her friends are expected to earn for their households as well. During this time, citizens are eligible to work in the commercial businesses located at the north and west ends of Hoboken if they are at least sixteen years of age. Although too young to work, the girls know a pharmacist who will forge them birth certificates for twenty-five cents. Iona gets Eva a job working at Castle Point in an office building. There, Eva learns to work large telephone boards as an operator and take notes on the professors' research. She documents the process while returned vets are administered Rorschach and other such tests.

Not to be outdone by Iona, Eva works a second job too. She sweeps innumerable floorboards for Karo Syrup, a baking supply company whose fragrant pancake syrup can be smelled for blocks. Karo is located on a floor of what will become the historic Lipton Tea Building on 15th Street. Besides maple-flavored syrup and Earl Grey tea, the Lipton Tea Building houses other businesses, like one that makes coconut candies and another that embroiders patches for the American soldiers' uniforms. This is also

The Lipton Tea Building, renamed Hudson Tea Building, is today known for its luxury condos, white-collar price tags, and famous tenants.

where Antonia works, endlessly sewing patch after patch while Eva works with her broom on another floor.

Wonder Bread and Hostess Cupcakes are in the neighborhood too. The drivers and other factory workers manage their own side hustle. Locals wait in the evenings at the shipping bay for delivery trucks to find their way back to base. The unsold, spoiling stock of baked goods are then dispatched with. One dollar nabs twenty loaves of day-old Wonder Bread. Eva and the rest of the neighborhood children drag wagons full of the bread all the way back to the Jefferson Street apartment in the Italian district, down in the opposite end of town.

As the United States becomes more entrenched in Europe, metal is rationed around the nation. Shortages in raw materials limit the ability to manufacture luxury items. 1942 sees the wider introduction of refrigerators, but, unfortunately, the distribution of these state-of-the-art appliances is stunted by the War. In order to purchase a refrigerator, a family has to be placed on a purchaser list, forced to wait their turn for an available model.

Until 1942, food freshness was the sole jurisdiction of the ice box. An ice box, however, is only good for keeping food fresh for a day. Nonperishable versions for all sorts of regular goods are a necessity. Milk, for example, is made from a stay-fresh powder called Palma. The ice box also needs to be filled with ice periodically each day. Under the ice box sits a pan that collects the melting ice. It needs emptying three times a day, or it spills over. Eva hates when she returns from school and steps in a chilly puddle with her wool socks. However, sympathy is hard to come by. It is usually Eva's job to empty the pan, and therefore it is her job to mop up the spill.

Despite all this, the Ovarsi girls are not subdued by the demands of wartime America. They still find ways to feed their passion for performing. Thirteen-year-old Eva finds that music has been missing in her life ever since the FBI's intrusion on her last performance. Iona is less interested, but always supportive of activities that keep Eva busy and out of trouble. The girls join the Potterton Chorus in Jersey City. Eva's vocals continue to improve beyond the average tween yelper, and everyone around her realizes it. She is developing into something special.

The Potterton Chorus is made up of one hundred men and women of all ages. The chorus performs various genres of songs, and each performance may include dancing and instruments, to create a rich and unique experience for the audience. The girls perform with them every

Saturday for two years. They get to travel all over the New York metro area. Most often, the chorus holds shows at public spaces or government-owned venues such as parks and armories. The regional radio station 94.9 WHOM broadcasts the chorus' weekly performance from Journal Square in Jersey City. The segment is sweetly named "Children's Hour."

The Ovarsis aren't the only family looking for an outlet. In Hoboken during the war, there are clubs segregated by gender and, unofficially, by race. Members wear jackets with the club and logos on them. The embossed club jackets are expensive, costing upwards of fifteen dollars. There are many clubs engendering different interests. Scrappy men's clubs include The Satan's Club, The Clover Club, The Rappers, and The Golden Boys. Young women choose from The Baby Dolls, The Coca-Colas, and The Starlets, to name a few. Linda Ovarsi, now a preteen, is president and founder of the Coca-Cola Club. There is no affiliation with the beverage company, but the members spend most of their time sharing laughs and boy talk over the sugary drink. Iona is a member of The Starlets Club, and Eva also belongs to The Young Starlets. She happily sings, dances, and twirls with other small girls with big dreams.

CHAPTER 5

"IF A MAN IS ALIVE, THERE IS ALWAYS DANGER THAT HE
MAY DIE, THOUGH THE DANGER MUST BE ALLOWED TO BE
LESS IN PROPORTION AS HE IS DEAD-AND-ALIVE TO BEGIN
WITH. A MAN SITS AS MANY RISKS AS HE RUNS."
— HENRY DAVID THOREAU, 'WALDEN'

A short while after the US enters WWII, the tide of the war turns, and things in the mainland begin changing rapidly. The Ovarsi family feel happy, upbeat, and optimistic for the first time in years. In recent weeks money seems to be coming in more easily, and families all over town are looking to expand and improve their lives. The 73 Jefferson Street apartment is feeling all too cramped, so, always the wise investor, Gustavo buys an eight-family, four-story building deep in the Italian district on Jackson Street. The entire building is six-thousand dollars: a substantial sum, but Gustavo has kept the family's finances secret while amassing the down payment. The Ovarsis convert and live on the entire first floor. Weightlifters use the basement as a gym, and the apartments on the second and third floors are rented out to other tenants.

Storefronts have new names, industry is growing, and more products than ever are available for the middle class to purchase. Even the shoeshine boy on the block is gaining more customers than his little hands can keep up with. The economic engine of the United States seems to be turning over. The Atlantic and Pacific Store at 9th and Washington, later rebranded and known everywhere simply as A&P, holds butter and ground coffee by the brick. Coffee companies such as 8 O'Clock and Red Circle sell their novel product for twenty-five cents and thirty-five cents respectively.

The Ovarsis are finally at the top of the waitlist to buy a refrigerator! The Norge-brand refrigerator stands tall at five feet high. This luxurious home appliance includes a small freezer cubby in the top right corner with enough space to forge twelve full-sized ice cubes.

The local government requires gas lines to be run to each building in the metropolitan area. Dangerous coal stoves, such as the one used to burn Eva's fascist duds, are prohibited. The new stove has four gas jets that are lit with a long matchstick, and a water heater is installed next to the stove. Hot water! This has been a dream of Eva's for as long as she can remember. And now that the Ovarsis have renovated the first floor for themselves, the bathroom is even inside the apartment. This is special and fairly unique among Hoboken apartment buildings, because floors with multiple residents—such as all of the floors above the Ovarsi home—have to share a communal bathroom. Eva and Iona feel very fortunate to have their own, private bathroom.

There is a washing machine too—*has the turning of the War ushered in the future?* the Ovarsi children wonder to themselves—little more than a drum that has to be manually filled with water from the heater. Then the washer needs emptying before being filled again with clean water. Compared to the involvement necessary for cleaning clothes before, however, this is no inconvenience at all. To the contrary, this is luxury. Antonia sings while doing housework. The clean laundry still dries on a clothing line, but wooden clothing pins have moved on to metal pins. Unfortunately, they regularly fail and let clothes fall to the ground. Not all innovations are improvements! Electric irons are still many years off. Flat irons still require heating on the stove before pressing. The process is lengthy, but it's a better time for middle-class Americans and Antonia is glowing with delight.

The furniture store is now carrying television sets in the window. Pedestrians stop to watch the glowing boxes stacked high through the thick pane, crowding the sidewalk until the store owner has to disperse the mob. Televisions are so new and so popular that the store is forced to maintain a another waitlist for excited future TV consumers.

Gustavo goes on the list and finally receives the long-awaited call months later. The newest models are ready for him to look at! The Ovarsis' first television set, an Olympic TV, is a small box with a round, nine-inch screen. Gustavo was nervous to spend the money, but his excitement won him over. The day they get their first TV, Eva, Gus Jr., and Linda take a

Left to right: Eva, Linda, Mario [kneeling, wearing altar boy vestment], and Antonia on a rooftop

wagon to Bergerline Ave., Jersey City. Antonia and Gustavo bought the TV beforehand to pick up later, since they do not own a car. The young teens walk up the Palisades along a steep winding road. They roll the set home, plug it in, and connect the rabbit ears to the back of the TV. Eva trembles with anticipation. Unfortunately, Antonia and Gustavo aren't home yet, and the kids cannot crack how to turn it on. Even while staring at a blank screen in a wooden box, they feel rich.

Reality for the Ovarsi household, however, soon takes an unexpected turn for the worse. Just as a new normal seems to have been achieved after years and years of struggle, tragedy condemns the family. On December 5, 1942, Eva rushes home from school to babysit the younger siblings, so that Gustavo and Antonia can work. Always saving for something, Eva's parents are taking on extra hours to pay for a glamorous holiday dinner. Eva gets home late and scrambles to get settled, pick up some clutter, and help undress Rosemary from her school clothes. Mario runs out to play before Eva is ready. What seems like only a few fleeting moments later, Eva hears a vehicle skid in the street below and a violent commotion ensue.

Mario, who just celebrated his ninth birthday on November 11, was outside playing ball in the street with the kids in the neighborhood, gleefully touting his Scouts uniform. One of the older boys whacked a long fly ball down the boulevard and nudged plucky Mario to run the bases in his stead. Running, running, Mario swung his arms and lifted his legs hard to move from one designated base to the next.

"Car!" the centerfielder declared.

The two teams picked up any gear lying around and moved to one side of the street or another, but not Mario. Laughing wildly, not realizing the game had been paused to make way for the passing truck, Mario grinned wide as he rounded third base and headed to home plate. The heating oil truck revved its engine as it sped through the cleared ballfield and the driver gave a quick nod at the boys on the sidewalk. The cobblestone street is familiar to all the kids on the block, but it often trips up the less surefooted. It has been the cause of innumerable scuffed knees and scraped palms. Right outside the Ovarsi apartment stoop, near the corner of Jackson and 3rd Street, Mario stumbled and fell on the lumpy cobblestone.

The sound of the uneven street would have been deafening in the cabin of the lumbering truck. The driver would not have even known that he hit anything, had the ball players not screamed in horror at that very moment.

"STOP!" echoes between the row homes.

Seconds later, a neighbor boy jets up the stairs to tell Eva that Mario is caught in the wheel well of the utility truck.

Barely able to process the news, Eva runs out of the apartment building, skipping as many stairs as her small stride allows, and pulls her bloodied but still-breathing younger brother out from under the truck. His light body dangles limp in her cradling arms. Eva kneels crying in the street as Mario struggles to take in air. He is incapable of saying anything, and Eva is too hysterical and panicked to comprehend anything she hears. She holds her younger brother as he slips out of consciousness and passes away there in her arms.

Antonia and Gustavo are not far. They each return home to the cacophony of ambulance sirens, police cruisers, and medical personnel. Their prayers are not answered that day. It *was* one of their children—and Mario's death changes the family forever.

The following week is harrowing for many. All the Scout leaders from surrounding troops attend Mario's agonizing funeral and escort his casket to the burial plot. The Boy Scouts honor him with a three-gun salute as the casket descends into its final resting place in Flower Hill Cemetery of North Bergen.

In the immediate aftermath of the accident, lawyers visit the house on a couple of occasions to get the family to sue the trucking company, the oil provider, the driver… anyone.

"I don't want no money," Gustavo says. "My son is dead. Money won't change that."

They never file any charges.

Antonia blames herself and soon falls into a deep depression. She never cries, but sits silent and stares blankly, watching life continue on without her involvement. From then on, she pays far less attention to her other children and begins to drink heavily to numb the loss. Why did she think work was more important than guarding her children? Hadn't she sworn her vigilance after the loss of Mimi and Minna?

"If I had only been home to watch my babies…" she wonders incessantly.

Gustavo takes the loss hard too. Over time, his drinking also gets out of hand, and his temper becomes legendary. The Ovarsi children no longer spend much time at home if they can help it.

Gus Jr. is clearly confused by his older brother's death. The stress and anxiety he feels causes him to act out violently and even to lose his hair prematurely. By the time he turns eleven years old, his hair has thinned noticeably, and he is sent to an all-boys school to introduce some discipline and structure into his daily routine. But matters are made worse by the bullying he experiences there. The family decides he will be better off home-schooled from then on, which means Iona is yet again relied upon to take a major role in raising her siblings.

Gus Jr. will later find his outlet as a trained boxer. He will learn from fighters who frequent the gym in the basement of their building and will lose himself in his training for hours each day.

CHAPTER 6

"WHO YOU ARE TOMORROW BEGINS WITH WHAT YOU DO TODAY."
— TIM FARGO

When money and jobs are scarce and many children's parents have not yet assimilated, education is not seen as a priority. Eva's friends are dropping out of school all around her. Not all of them are able to get jobs that pay more than a few dollars per day. Eva doesn't want to be stuck with bunch of "do-nothing" friends, wasting their days just hanging around. She has five close friends until high school, where they break up and go their own ways. All five girls later leave school, but Eva continues on.

Iona is the biggest pusher. She wants Eva to graduate and become a top model. At some point, she figured that if Eva was going to continue to break into her now-locked closet and steal her clothes day after day, they might as well embrace her passions. This makes dropping out even more tempting, because modeling begins early. Eva has matured into a stunning young woman. Her thick auburn hair is always tamed, which brings attention to her striking hazel eyes and subtly perfect smile. The thought of getting paid to take pictures full-time is starting to sound very attractive. Eva can see the hope and excitement in Iona's face each and every time she brings it up. They spend late nights talking in the dark about what they could accomplish. Oftentimes, Eva just keeps quiet, staring into the darkness.

"If you think modeling is so great, why don't you do it?" she tells Iona in her head.

Iona probably would, but for one objective and hardline standard that she has no control over. She stands a mere five feet, three inches, which is too short by one inch to model.

Eva is embarrassed by Iona's persistence, but it is done out of earnest support. Iona isn't jealous... not really. Holding the title of big sister is important in the 1940s. She is the second mother of the household, the other head of the family, and all the siblings know it. When she instructs Eva to walk the younger ones to school while she works, Eva listens. That means something that not even modeling can give her.

Besides, Iona has dreams of her own. By the time she turns eighteen, Iona has become enamored with the notion of becoming a pilot. She has seen the recruitment posters and wants to join the Women's Airforce Service and become a WASP. She really is Rosie the Riveter. However, there is one small problem: Iona doesn't know how to fly. But Eva is about to get another education, this one in how to network. Iona meets a man who has his own airstrip in the Poconos through her work at the shipyards. He takes pleasure in teaching Iona how to soar above the clouds in an open cockpit, a Piper J-3 Cub. Every Saturday, she dresses like Amelia Earhart, secures her blonde-dyed hair to the side with gold-plated bobby pins, and drives Eva in her convertible to Pennsylvania. Free flying lessons are worth spending time with a guy Iona is cool on.

Further complicating Iona's dream is her age. Unfortunately, eighteen is too young to join any of the women's armed services units that have opened to volunteers amid World War II. All five branches of the military have female-only units, open to able-bodied women between the ages of twenty-one and thirty-five with varying degrees of education or work experience. There are the Women's Army Corps (WAC), the Women's Accepted Volunteer Emergency Service (WAVES), the Women's Airforce Service Pilots (WASP), the Marine Corps Women's Reserve, and the Coast Guard Women's Reserve (SPARS). Although each female service member is relegated to non-combat roles, their volunteerism is invaluable to the war effort. They free up military doctors, engineers, mechanics, cargo pilots, and many others to enter the theater of war.

Of course, no technicality is going to keep the Ovarsi girls from trying to get what they want. Eva sees the passion and dedication Iona holds for flying and for her country, and she wants to help any way she can. Iona's patriotism is infectious, though not necessarily uncommon. The Hoboken youth are all still incredibly busy working to earn money to help the household or, in some ancillary way, to support the national war effort. Women in particular have shouldered enormous responsibility during the war, while some 17.5 million men have been called to arms halfway around the globe.

Yet it is not a tightly-held secret that the government is limiting the roles of women in the armed services to those presumed to be safe or somehow "appropriate" for women. To further discriminate, the age minimum is higher in most respects than for men. Does the government assume women over the age of twenty-one are more physically capable, or are they expecting only women with weak marriage prospects to volunteer? The female officers hold no station or authority higher than any male counterpart, regardless of rank.

So Eva uses her voice, only this time it is the written word. Never afraid to jump into a space occupied by adults, she sits down and pens a succinct editorial for the *New York Daily News*, Voice of the People.

"EVA GROWS IMPATIENT

Hoboken, N.J.: These girls of 21 and up who are in the armed services are no better than we girls of 14-17. Most of us want to quit school and get busy winning this war: so how about some junior WACs, junior WAVES, etc.?

Eva Ovarsi"

This is Eva's rallying cry: that a teenage girl has the fight in her to help Uncle Sam. She notifies all that she is not alone and is not to be babied. Eva never expects the U.S. government to enlist fourteen-year-olds to deploy to active war zones, but her intentions are clear. She wants to do any small part to help the men-at-arms and to bring the country out of war… as victors. Many of her friends have, after all, already dropped out of school, which means they are available for the country.

In the end, however, all of this hard work and outcry fails to erode one immovable fact: as in modeling, Iona is not tall enough to be a pilot. She does not meet the service's height requirement of 5'4". But she bears it up, as Iona always does, and continues taking her flights in the Poconos.

Although inspired by her sister's commitment to their country, and having acted as an inspiration to others through her op-ed submission, Eva is continuously called in another direction. Over the years, her singing talent has grown, along with her enthusiasm for performing. Now, at fifteen, she gets her chance to sing in front of a large crowd at the famed Fabian Theater.

The Fabian is a beautifully adorned and constructed live performance theater with thirty-five hundred seats[3], set in the heart of Hoboken's downtown. It sits across the street from City Hall. Two Potterton Chorus members are selected by their peers to try out for the theater's amateur night. On a Saturday, a representative of the Fabian Theater scouts the Potterton Chorus. Eva wows him with her classic voice. She is able to fearlessly project without the help of a microphone, and her rendition of "The Blonde Sailor" by The Andrew Sisters blows the scout away. She is exactly what the Fabian wants—a raw talent who can make the audience swoon with the pure emotion behind her vocals. She nails the audition, as does fellow Chorus member Florence Smith.

Eva's now fourteen-year-old sister Linda is a great promoter. Her electric personality attracts everyone in Hoboken, from every corner of town. She makes sure that the theater is packed for Eva's debut. Eva is aware that Linda has been canvassing Hoboken in her signature roller skates, but she is taken aback by the packed house on the night of her performance. This is a record-high attendance night for the theater.

Eva and Florence watch act after act perform before them. Their block of songs is scheduled to second-to-last, with four before them. The girls sit backstage, primping in the makeup mirrors. A single small window is kept open with the help of a book. The temperature in the room inches closer to 90 degrees, and the cool air is a welcome, desperate relief.

There is a first time for everything, and this is the first time the fearless Rookie's nerves get the best of her during the time leading up to her performance. But when she looks out over the crowd of friendly faces, Potterton Chorus singers, high school friends, and girls' club members, nervousness falls away to excitement. Eva is adorned in a gorgeous yellow Chantilly lace gown that was happily lent to her by Iona for the big night. Eva loves this dress. She feels beautiful and sophisticated in the snug comfort of the long, form-fitting sleeves, and she is proud of her smooth skin and delicate neck exposed by the scooping neckline.

Eva and Florence are scheduled to alternate songs before concluding with a stirring duet. Florence steps out and positions herself behind the stationary microphone. The songs that the girls are singing were supplied by the chorus and have already been sung by each of them dozens of times.

The Fabian Theater in Hoboken (not to be mistaken for the Paterson, NJ, theater of the same name) was located on the corner of Newark Street and Washington Street. Built in 1928, The Fabian Theater was a 3,500-seat marvel that played host to live performances from headliners such as Frank Sinatra and Al Jolson before later screening movies. The Fabian languished in the '60s and finally closed for good in 1965.[4] In 1968, it was torn down and replaced by a rotation of groceries and retail chains.

Yet Florence has such a beautiful voice, it takes Eva away. She nearly forgets that once Florence's first song is over, it is her own turn to perform.

Florence's final note is drowned out by loud applause. She turns, waves at the crowd, and approaches Eva offstage.

"You're UP!"

A quick breath, and Eva is off. She walks down the long, wide stage to take her position behind the mic. The curtains, heavy velvet in a burgundy color, are already open. Eva will be singing upbeat War songs, her wheelhouse. The welcome clapping from the audience has not fully died down before Eva breaks into "Johnny Comes Marching Home Again."

The crowd loves it. Eva can see beyond the bright stage lights into the seats, where her father is sitting proudly but quietly with Linda, who is clapping wildly with the rest of the theater. With both girls feeling ever more empowered by their strong performances so far, Florence joins Eva at center stage to perform their duet, "I'll Never Smile Again," a hometown favorite by Frank Sinatra.

Earlier, Iona snuck backstage to provide additional support and to make sure the entire show went off without a hitch. During the final cast bow, while the entire audience screams and claps, Eva can see Iona jumping up and down offstage. It is a great feeling. The performance was a true success.

In September 1945, the full surrender of the Axis of Evil comes. World War II ends, and the troops return home in droves. Shipfuls of happy sailors and war veterans fill the streets of Hoboken each week. Along the Hudson River sits Bethlehem Steel and Todd's Shipyard, so the area served as a port of embarkation where warships could be fixed and new parts were forged. This means that seeing sailors is not new to the city, but now the streets seem electric. The local taverns especially reap the benefits. The energy lifts everyone's spirits and continues the optimism that America has been witnessing since the tide of the war turned in 1942. With the dark storm cloud of global conflict cleared away from her heart, Eva turns and looks to her own horizons.

CHAPTER 7

"YOUR NEED FOR ACCEPTANCE CAN MAKE YOU INVISIBLE
IN THIS WORLD. DON'T LET ANYTHING STAND IN THE WAY
OF THE LIGHT THAT SHINES THROUGH THIS FORM. RISK
BEING SEEN IN ALL OF YOUR GLORY."
— JIM CARREY

The war is over, and, surrounded by the many influences of the Big Apple, Eva begins to seriously explore her artistry in music. Her lithe build, clear olive-toned skin, and gentle smile attract attention even when she is not performing. She meets a nice young Italian boy who takes an immediate liking to her, not unlike Iona's Pennsylvania airman. Emanuel "Manny" Vigiano is an usher at Radio City Music Hall. He gets Eva passes every week and leaves them at the side door for her. With these tickets, Eva has a special seat reserved in the mezzanine. When the show is over, she goes downstairs to the lobby and sits on the red velvet benches. She waits for him to finish with his duties.

Working in "the biz" has other perks too. Manny takes Eva to bars and clubs, despite the fact that she is underage. In fact, they go to some clubs even though Eva is not of the right gender! She loves pushing her luck, so one evening after Manny's shift, the duo enters McSorley's Irish Pub, the oldest bar in Manhattan. Not only is Eva too young, but McSorley's is a men-only saloon at this time. Female guests chaperoned by male patrons are permitted to sit in a designated area toward the rear of the bar. There they are served something to eat. While the men guzzle mason jars of either the house-brewed "light" or "dark" beers, always two at a time, the ladies gossip and nibble on the humble cuisine du jour. The women are spoiled with choice: either a liver sandwich or a plate of cheese and saltine crackers. No more is to be expected from a venue proud of the sawdust on the ground and ever-growing mounds of dust on the neglected brass chandeliers. Nevertheless, the ladies sitting beside Eva relish their time out. With eyes wide and ambitions growing, Eva Ovarsi has arrived as a metropolitan girl, and she is not going to wait to make her mark for much longer.

New York City, its suburbs in northern New Jersey, and especially Hoboken have been hotbeds of musical talent since the 1920s. Eva is growing up among some of the greatest entertainers of all time. Young men and women who will soon become household names are living all around the Ovarsi household, within an earshot of the Square Mile. One of the most famous entertainers of the era, and Hoboken's most beloved son, is Frank Sinatra. Eva knows Francis Sinatra from his singing around the neighborhood. In 1935, the very beginning of his career, Sinatra joined with the 3 Flashes to compose the Hoboken Four. This occurred serendipitously after the trio and the solo singer both performed well during competing auditions for the Major Bowes Amateur Hour radio show. Major Bowes, and possibly Sinatra's mother, Dolly, concocted a plan and convinced the trio to absorb Frank as a member of their band.

The other members of the quartet are James ("Jimmy Skelly") Petrozelli, who plays the guitar; Patrick ("Patty Prince") Principe behind the drums; and Fred ("Freddie Tamby") Tamburro, who provides bass. The group practices behind Eva's house, much to her delight. When Frank and the boys perform across the Hudson River at the Paramount Theater, nearly every teen in the region plays hooky. With one dollar in their pockets, students pay thirty-five cents for a bus ticket into the city and fifty cents to get into the theater. This leaves a young audience member with fifteen cents off a dollar, plenty for snacks and pop.

Show business is a way out of the grind for immigrant families in America. The Irish and the Germans monopolize political control in New Jersey and New York, which leaves the Italians few clear avenues for quick societal advancement. Even Sinatra's father changed his name to Marty O'Brien so that he could box, live, and conduct business in the Irish areas of town. But talent is a currency that cannot be easily manipulated. It is a ticket to the fast lane, a special ride into high society.

One afternoon, Eva sits on the familiar red velvet benches while the matinee show's final attendee leaves Radio City through a row of double doors. Eva is used to the routine and does not mind the time to herself. But something odd is stirring. Beautiful girls, long and lean with strong feminine silhouettes, are darting around the venue. Never too shy to remain ignorant for long, Eva politely stops one of the ladies.

"Hello! Excuse me, hello, what's going on?"

"They are casting some new girls for the Rockettes!" the hopeful candidate answers. Her glee quickly sours into concern. Eva could be her competition.

Eva knows how to dance, and her self-confidence is only getting stronger by the day, so she figures she'll try. Eva finds her way to a casting desk and puts her name down on a sign-in sheet. Then she waits to be called. At sixteen, she gambles on her pretty face and strong presence to attract attention away from the fact that she is donning daywear, ill-suited for a high-energy dance tryout.

Eva's name and number are called. It is time to put her best foot forward, and she does exactly that. Eva walks on stage with a long and deliberate stride. She treats every moment on stage as if the casting directors were paying spectators on opening night of the season spectacular. The raised, lacquered planks are her catwalk. She keeps her eyes wide in spite of the glaring stage lamps. With a broad stage smile, Eva introduces herself to the directors and instructs the musicians to begin her "prepared routine." Never unprepared, Eva just happens to have a little dance number memorized.

The casting directors love it, but they can tell she isn't eighteen years of age, which in 1946 is a requirement for being in the Rockettes. "Young lady, how old are you?"

"Eighteen," she answers assertively.

A reactionary chuckle forces a smile across the director's face. "No, you're not!"

She lies again, feigning no less confidence than before. "Okay… I am seventeen!"

"Miss, you've got what it takes, but you are too young." He looks down at his clipboard before raising his head and addressing Eva once more. "Come back next year, and you'll have a job. NEXT!"

Manny finishes up his duties. Eva cannot hold in her excitement. Manny wants to celebrate the burgeoning star he calls his girlfriend, so he decides to pull out all the stops and escorts Eva to the only restaurant he can think of that is suitable for a starlet of the stage: a staple of Broadway and the Theater District called Sardi's Restaurant. Eva has never been to Sardi's, and she knows the menu is expensive. Neither of them has much money, but that does not stop them. The couple share a shrimp cocktail and a large ice cream soda for about five dollars.

Eva is over the moon. This is her first experience in a New York City restaurant, following the most important moment of her young life. She has received the push she needs—the affirmation that the star quality she feels twisting inside of her, the anxious energy looking for an opening to burst forth, is the marker of true skill.

Eva does not, however, return to try out for the Rockettes the following year, since she is still too young.

Eva adores singing, but Iona, always loving and supportive, finally convinces her to get out from behind the sound booth, where she has been singing jingles for radio commercials whenever the opportunity arises. Iona knows of a modeling school that happens to be connected to the hotel that hosts the charm and etiquette classes she attends. The renowned New York modeling school is accepting freshman enrollees for the following semester.

Beauty and grace, intrigue and excitement, safety and support: these tenets, among many others, are the superlatives used to describe The Barbizon Hotel. So much more than a modeling school, The Barbizon Hotel is the pinnacle of female talent development in all matters. Built in the late 1920s for the purpose of providing a safe haven for ascendant women, the hotel is an architectural masterpiece melding Italian Renaissance, Islamic, and Gothic design styles. It features a luxurious multi-story atrium, an Olympic-sized swimming pool, squash courts, a gymnastics center, and instructional areas for models, actresses, and those pursuing the charms required for a life as the madam of a millionaire's estate. The Barbizon Hotel houses seven hundred young women on any given day. Many girls are dropped off by affluent families during the winter months to be groomed by the Barbizon etiquette school. Other residents are talented starlets being kept safe from the ravages of the real world. The hotel also provides asset protection for other major talent agencies, with a vault housing precious jewels. Simply referred to as Barbizons by the insiders, it serves as the preeminent preparatory school for all types of successful "modern" women.

Buoyed by her success in the Rockettes audition, Eva agrees to enroll in the modeling school. She and Iona will end up paying their own ways through modeling and charm school, respectively. They cannot afford to be full-time residents alongside many of their peers. Instead, the sisters stay many weekends with other girls who are renting rooms. But they don't mind this—far from it. Where others see an impediment, Eva and Iona take pride in besting the harshness of reality. They have survived a voyage from another continent so that they may fulfill their potential, and the Ovarsi sisters are emboldened to take on any obstacle that stands in their way.

Eva's headshot

CHAPTER 8

"NEVER WAS ANYTHING GREAT ACHIEVED WITHOUT DANGER."
— NICCOLO MACHIAVELLI

Two years have now passed since the Axis' surrender in 1945, and Hoboken's Mayor Fred DeSapio is looking to celebrate America's achievement and Hoboken's support of the successful war effort. His people are planning a month of festivities, topped off with a big parade marching down Washington Street, straight through the heart of the city. Members of the city council think it would be a great idea to crown a pageant winner as part of this March of Progress. So the festival directors establish the first ever Miss Hoboken Beauty Pageant. The winner will be unveiled to the city during the parade.

The directors visit the high schools peppered throughout the city. All high school senior girls willing to participate are asked to appear at each school's auditorium, where they will showcase their talents, if they choose to, in front of the closed panel.

Demarest High School sits across a sprawling park from Our Lady of Grace Church, and is home to a seventeen-year-old Eva and her friends five days a week. They, along with Iona, are well-liked and popular. Eva has now been scrutinized on stage dozens of times. When the directors come to her school, she is waiting. They ask the girls to have a walk on the stage, present themselves, and perform a talent.

Once it is time for Eva Patricia Ovarsi to introduce herself, she takes all of the Barbizon classes she has been attending to task. She glides onto the stage with a refined walk, turns, and stands to greet the panel of judges with impeccable posture. After a brief, pleasant opening, she sings one of her early 1940s patriotic love songs. The judges adore her. Out of all the young ladies that try out across the city, only three contestants are picked for a final round of popular voting: Eva and two others.

This makes Eva, who knows she is popular at the school, excited. She is not one of the rich girls, and she does not host parties or show off fancy cars, but she seems a certain choice for this vote. The schools all take time out of first period to cast votes, and Eva clinches her place as the first and only Miss Hoboken.

October passes with Hoboken in a bustle all month long. It is no coincidence the final events take place on the 30th, Frank Sinatra Day, since Dolly Sinatra works very closely with the Mayor's office. Eva and the two pageant runners-up ride through the March of Progress parade atop a fire engine, smiling and waving to everyone watching. The weather, however, is horrible. Chilly rain cascades down on the parade and the onlookers. Eva's coiffed hair has flattened, and she attempts to hide behind her once-beautiful bouquet as the engine creeps down Washington.

Frank Sinatra has made a triumphant return to his hometown. He and his father, Marty the Fire Chief, ride together in a different fire engine. With onlookers clapping, children hollering, and emergency vehicles blaring their horns, it is nearly impossible to understand the mix of signals. Eva and the two runners-up are having the time of their lives, even with the rain, and they really get into character, waving and blowing dainty kisses. They have no idea that a few vehicles behind them, an unhappy crowd is actually booing Sinatra. Their words are downright vitriolic as they throw trash and rotten food at him, angry because he never gave Hoboken any credit for his star power. Frank Sinatra was, until this moment, unaware that his greatest hit, "New York, New York," created a seething jealousy among a vocal minority of the older, lifelong Hoboken residents.

Soon after her coronation as Miss Hoboken, Eva is picked up by Clyde Matthews Agency, a relatively new agency with a youth model division situated in Midtown East. Agency owner Clyde Matthews looks for more than just skinny arms and legs. To Mr. Matthews, his talent are the Matthews Madonnas. He used the term "supermodel" as early as 1943, when he envisioned a glorious future for the industry, saying, "The model

Frank Sinatra Day, October 30, 1947

Left to right: Martin Sinatra [partially seen], Dolly Sinatra, Mayor Fred DeSapio, Miss Hoboken runner-up, Frank Sinatra, Eva, and Commissioner George Fitzpatrick

will be… not just an attractive doll, but a living, speaking, acting, charming woman of international society… She will be a supermodel."

Eva is excelling in her modeling school curriculum and loves the incredible experience at this preeminent agency. She never gets lost in the excitement, however, knowing that she needs to massage her image if she is going to make it big. It is time to rebrand with a new stage name, one that will propel her career past the point being reached by other Italian girls from the tenements. Eva decides on "Eve Aris."

Clyde Matthews Agency keeps Eve Aris very busy. Her latest gig is with another industry newcomer, a clothing design team that goes by the name Evan-Picone. Business partners Charles Evans and Joseph Picone demand perfection for the industry "first look" Eva has been plucked to walk. The dress manufacturer is showcasing some new designs for a collection of buyers. As is to be expected, the first look showcase is vital to the burgeoning fashion house. The all-male band of tailors, textile specialists, and design students are hurriedly but effectively fitting each dress to the models' curves.

With returning veterans flooding back stateside, there has been a distinct change in the workplace dynamic between men and women. Young, jaded men, many of whom have known only war in their adulthoods, are integrating back into a world that had to continue running in their absence. War, alcohol, and solitude are what they are accustomed to. Meanwhile, women have gained more power in the workplace, and they are loath to give it up. In the fashion industry, gender relationships are further complicated by the fact that a model's personal space is not observed. This is out of necessity. The Evan-Picone employees must do everything they can to tailor the dress prototypes snugly to each individual model. A sensitive model is an unemployed model. This is true despite the standard of professionalism being exhibited in this day.

Since this is not a runway show, the performance is held at the Evan-Picone factory in Jersey City. All of the models are young and relatively inexperienced. Eva has never been in a first look before and, as always, is eager to impress. The dresses are uncomfortable. They are not finished, tailored pieces. Instead they are pinned and pieced together with the hope that they will look stunning for the next hour only.

Eva completes walking in the first of three dresses planned for her to model that afternoon. She is about to showcase her second when a voice rings out.

"No, no, no! Miss Aris, please, Miss Aris, this is all wrong. Will someone please get over here and fix Eve Aris' dress?! It's lumpier than a sack of potatoes. It's falling all wrong. Come take care of this; we cannot have this." Then another issue grabs Joseph Picone's attention, and he skips off to handle the crisis.

A dapper young man in his twenties with a neat part in his wavy hair jogs toward Eva.

"Hello, Eve. This will only take a minute." His eyes dart between Charles Evans and Eva. His forehead glistens with small beads of sweat.

As the man maneuvers around Eva's hips and midriff, fumbling as he attempts to begin pinning and rethreading small sections of fabric to lay flush against her figure, she notices that his shirt covers strong shoulders and a deep tan. His hair is thick and a very dark brown.

Eva lifts her arms to give her aide room to work. "Watch your hands," she warns.

"My hands aren't what I'm watching, Eve," he quips.

Then Charles, struggling to keep his composure during the important showcase, starts yelling. "Who the hell are you? Get outta here! I could have you fired for doing that!"

The young man spins around, startled. "I was just trying to help out around here. You guys were in a jam, and I was free, so I thought I'd, uh…"

"You sweep floors. Are you kidding me? Get the hell outta here and finish your job. You do what you do, and let the pattern makers do what they do!" Charles's rigid hands dance along with his outburst as if he wants to physically carry his employees to their proper place in the factory. Veins protrude wherever his skin is exposed.

Steamed at the lack of professionalism she is now experiencing, Eva enters the verbal trouncing with a heavy local accent. "Get off me. Don't you dare touch me. Don't ever touch me! You're not allowed to lay a finger on me!"

"So I suppose a date is outta the question?" the young man interrupts with a smart smile. He is lucky his employer does not catch his proposal. Otherwise, Charles may have ordered him to go home.

Eva's small fists are clenched in frustration, but there is nothing more to do. She is there to work as well. It is time that she gets back to it.

The young man retreats to the rear of the factory. Eve Aris takes a few deep breaths as two stylists replace the sweeper. Then off she goes, smiling her broad, white smile for the buyers.

A few passes with dress two and three conclude her work for the day. Eva and the rest of the models are thanked by the Evan-Picone team.

It has been a good day. Tired from stress and waking early in the morning, the ladies throw on light coats and gather their small purses from the dressing room. As the last of the girls leaves, the door is eased open by a large, heavy man in a suit. The exiting models nearly run right into him, bouncing off his imposing chassis. He has a light complexion, pockmarked skin, dark hair, and a large nose. He wears thick glasses and a permanent scowl. His gray suit appears and smells worn and is in need of laundering.

"Please excuse me, ladies." The man moves into the room.

The models apologize to him and look back at Eva as they shuffle through the door. Eva returns their glances, confused.

"Great job today, ladies. Really terrific," the man exclaims—and then he closes the door behind the other girls.

Eva is alone.

"Ms. Aris, am I right, Ms. Eve Aris?"

"Hello. Yes. Who are you?"

"I'm a buyer for Macy's. I was watching you. I liked what I saw."

His glare smothers Eva's body. Her anxiety is building, and her chest tightens, making it hard to breathe. "Now, look, Mister, you are not allowed in here."

"Now, now, Ms. Aris, that is no way to make friends in this business." He moves a step closer. "And I can be a really good friend."

The bright makeup bulbs illuminate his pockmarked cheeks.

"Did you hear me? I said get out of here!" Eva's heart pounds. Blood flees her fingertips. Her skin begins to tingle and itch. "Not today! Get out of here! You are not allowed!"

The intruder's eyes widen and dart back toward the exit. Eva is yelling loudly. This will not end well for him if he pushes on.

"Calm down now, Ms. Aris, this was all just a misunderstanding," he says, as if to hypnotize her into believing it. Without looking, he reaches back to palm the brass doorknob, deftly withdrawing through the dressing room door. He leaves Eva clutching the vanity behind her as she struggles to catch her breath.

Eva's headshot

CHAPTER 9

"ALL LIFE'S A RISK, THAT'S WHAT MAKES IT INTERESTING." — MEGAN CHANCE, 'THE SPIRITUALIST'

The vets have been returning home for months, and unemployment is high, but Eva has found someone to take care of her. Henry Coradino— "Corky" to his pals—is a young, slightly naïve gentleman who treats Eva well. He drives her and her friends wherever they want to go. Henry is a university man, attending Seton Hall and studying business. Eva considers him to be a very good friend.

One evening, Eva accompanies him to a restaurant where friends and family are celebrating an anniversary. Eva does not care to pay attention to the details, but she is enjoying her time with Henry nonetheless. When they enter the restaurant, Eva catches the eyes of two men sitting at the bar, Ralph Grimaldi and Patrick "Patty" Kelly.

Patty is a well-known townie, a friend of everyone and no one. He is blonde, Irish, and an alcoholic among alcoholics. Ralph is Corky's friend who has returned from a storied stint in Western Europe as part of the 26th Infantry "Yankee" Division. His face has been toughened by war. His strong features and cinderblock jaw give way to soft, innocent eyes, and he has thick, dark hair, parted on the left side. Though Ralph and Corky are good friends, they share a friendly rivalry. They are always trying to get each other's women.

Patty and Ralph, for their part, could not be any more different.

However, both men are well on their way to being stone drunk.

Corky, always quick with an introduction, presents Eva to the men. "Eve, these are some of the ol' Secaucus boys! Patty, Ralph, please meet my girlfriend, Eve. She's a model."

Eva does not embarrass easily, but hates it when Corky puts her on the spot like this—and she never agreed to be anybody's girl! Half-flattered, half-put-off, Eva tightens her posture and gestures with her hand. "How do you do."

"Oh—she's a model, huh? What does she model... gloves?" A crooked grin peeks for a moment out of Ralph's face.

Eva says with a schoolteacher's resolve: "That's not very nice. But I'll get even with you someday for that."

Her glare says a lot more.

"Don't talk like that to her, Ralph." Corky speaks with confidence and sincerity, but his split-second hesitation has already been filled with Eva's assured retort.

"All right, all right, everyone just calm down." Ralph's hands are held up in relaxed surrender. The grin hasn't left his face, even as his eyes lock onto Eva's heavy cheekbones and deep hazel eyes.

Eva spins on the balls of her red slingback heels to face Corky. "It's time we join your family, don't you think, Henry?"

"Okay, fellas, we'll be seeing ya."

Ralph and Patty spare no time swiveling back toward their bourbon and beer as the handsome couple leave to greet the rest of the party guests.

"Corky?" Eva whispers now that the twosome is no longer within an earshot of the bar. "That Ralph fella looks familiar."

"You may have met him. He works at a garment center now."

Eva disagrees. "I don't think so."

So Corky tells her a little more about Ralph, who was inducted into the

Satan's Club after returning from service. The Club wears burgundy and white-colored clothing, but had no jackets at the time Ralph joined. They focused their attention on gambling and alcohol, with a favorite hangout called the Sky Club on Hudson Avenue. Ralph's industriousness led to him becoming President. He's been working to impose his vision on the group ever since. First, he made sure they had obligatory jackets like the other established clubs. Second, he's welcomed other returning veterans, reserving space for them in the Satan's Club. It is important to Ralph that the vets have a comfortable place to return to when they come home. In particular, Ralph is waiting for his brother, Larry Grimaldi, who is in the Sea Bees. Larry is stationed in Guam, and Ralph intends to keep the Satan's Club open until Larry comes home.

The anniversary gathering winds down. Corky grabs the couple's coats and hats, and they head toward the door, arm-in-arm. It has been a nice time, but Eva is distracted by her excitement for the coming weeks. She has landed a few more gigs and will be graduating Barbizon Modeling School soon. A party has been planned for her at the bowling alley later that month. All of her closest friends have committed to being there, and it is guaranteed to get pretty loose.

Before reaching the door, Eva thinks to take a look at the bar to see if Corky's friends are still sitting there. They are not. They must have relocated elsewhere to continue their bender.

Probably better off, Eva thinks to herself. She doesn't trust any man at face value, and certainly doesn't have any reason to trust these ones—even if they are Corky's friends.

The Playdrome Bowling Alley in Union is a favorite hangout for the teens and young adults of North Jersey. They serve drinks late into the night, providing the perfect opportunity for flirting and peacocking. It's the Tuesday night after Corky's family reunion, and Ralph, Patty, and Corky are going out. They hit up the Playdrome after stopping off for some Dewars first.

The Playdrome is packed, and everyone is having a good time. As eleven o'clock approaches, urgency sets in among the boys. Ralph has met Maria "Tootsie" Dellastratto and is looking to score her number. Tootsie is a pretty girl with small features and shoulder-length hair that she wears parted on the side and held behind her ears. She is Eva's best dancing buddy. Patty has spent his night waving down the bartender, and so is scrambling for just about anybody's number. Corky continues to slink around Eva.

Not surprisingly, Patty's drinks soon catch up with him. Ralph, a man of habit and control, has the crew climb into his car so he can drive them home. Tootsie is excited, but Eva just needs a ride. Corky sits shotgun alongside Ralph while the girls and Patty are left to sit snugly in the back.

Eva leans in close to Tootsie's ear and says, "That Patty Kelly looks like a friggin' wise guy. I am not sitting back there with him."

Unfortunately, she doesn't have much of a choice.

The night's libations hot on Patty's breath are aggravatingly apparent. He starts to feel out his chances with the pair of women. Not reading the cards well, he unartfully slides his hands where any five-year-old knows is inappropriate. "That's enough!" Eva screams and demands that Ralph pull over.

Though brash and cheeky at times, with a smart tongue, Ralph is still a gentleman. Obviously steamed with his Irish compatriot, he slams on the brakes and fishtails to a stop in the shoulder of Route 3. Then he swings a heavy hand behind him without leaving the driver seat. Firm from months of handling supply crates on the Red Ball Express, Ralph's hand knocks the drunk's head back into the passenger seat window.

Slightly confused and now squinting with his left eye, Patty plays dumb. "Ow! What the hell was that for?!"

"What, you want a knuckle sandwich? Why are you being such a wise guy? We are driving them home, for Christ's sake!"

Ralph declares the night over and proceeds to drop the passengers off. Patty gets dropped off with Tootsie near her house.

"I'll swing back after I drop off your friend here," Ralph calls out to Tootsie.

Corky is the third passenger to be let out and, after a goodbye to Eva, gives up his seat to her. Having gotten to know only a little bit about this Eva Patricia Ovarsi so far, Ralph tries to make their time in the car a little more comfortable by filling in the gaps of information that seemed to matter less only an hour before. It is an attempt to make up for any indiscretions that were forced upon the ladies in his care. Ralph is pleasantly surprised when Eva has a little more to say than the normal broad from

Hoboken.

The route he navigates to Eva's address is slightly more complicated than necessary, and Eva takes note without saying a word. Upon pulling up to the short Hoboken three-story, the two commence a kind goodbye. Seeing his window of opportunity coming to a close, and getting uncharacteristically clammy, Ralph tries to asks Eva one last question before throwing the car in first gear. His dry throat catches his words. He clears his throat to start again, but Eva is already exiting the long black sedan.

"Hey, Eve, whaddya say, can I call you sometime?"

Eva slams the passenger side door closed and leans into the open window. "No way. I don't know you. We've barely met!"

"I am a good man. I won't try nothin'."

Eva scans Ralph's face. Then she surrenders her telephone number.

It is a short twenty-foot walk from the street to the front door, and street lamps illuminate the whole block. Eva looks back toward the car, through the passenger seat window to Ralph, and she gives a flitting wave. Then she enters the tight foyer through a heavy front door.

Ralph hits the accelerator to head back to Tootsie's house.

Later that night, Tootsie calls Eva to gossip. Eva thinks Tootsie must want to brag about having Patty and Ralph over.

"Sooo," Tootsie says, "what happened in the car?"

"Nothing happened. Ralph dropped off Corky and then me."

"Did you give him any?"

"What? No! He did ask for my number. But he left me to go see you, ya know. I don't even know why he wanted it."

"No, no, you got it all wrong. He just scooped up Patty to bring him home. I already gave Patty my number earlier in the night. That's why Patty got dropped off near my parents' house."

"Oh my *Gawd*, Tootsie!"

Later that week, Ralph calls Eva to ask her out. Eva realizes this is her chance to get even with the wisecracking fellow.

"Meet me at the bowling alley this Saturday," she says. She has a photoshoot in NYC that will keep her working that weekend.

"Great, I'll see you there."

Come Saturday night, Ralph realizes after about an hour that he has been stood up. He grabs his things and speeds over to the address where he dropped Eva off a few nights earlier. After parking, he buzzes all three floors of the building.

Antonia answers the door. "Pronto, chi sei?"

But Ralph's Italian is weak, and Antonia's dialect does not match his native Sicilian.

Later, Eva arrives home.

"Ciao, Mamma! What an awful night! This photographer had no idea what he was doing, and Makeup wouldn't listen to me. I know what colors look good on me. It's *my* skin, after all…"

Antonia stands with her arms crossed. "Eva, un ragazzo arrivato a casa." She explains that a Sicilian boy named "Raf" had come looking for Eva. "Were you supposed to meet this boy? What's the matter with you? Che cosa fai?"

"He came here?" Eva realizes Ralph must have remembered where she lives from when he drove her home. "He came looking for me after I stood him up! Ugh! What a creep! And he knows where I live!"

CHAPTER 10

"FORTUNE SIDES WITH HIM WHO DARES."
— VIRGIL

It is the night of the Barbizon Modeling School graduation party for Eva and her friends. Upon entering the bowling alley, the sounds of laughter and shrill voices, tumbling bowling balls and crashing pins can be heard. Corky spots his friends from across a dozen lanes of bowling traffic and bounds in their direction to guide them inside.

Patty looks a bit dumbstruck. He chuckles to himself and swallows hard, gazing at the crowd. There are Barbizon models everywhere. He has never seen so many pretty girls, all of them dressed in full-length party gowns that are saturated with bold colors or decorated in lively prints. Frankly, most of the men patronizing Playdrome Bowling Alley have never been in the presence of so many beauties at once.

Patty skips off, hot on Corky's heels, leaving Ralph standing alone at the top of the stairs. Ralph usually dons thin-rimmed glasses, but has chosen to leave them behind tonight. His dark brown hair is carefully combed and his straight-razor shave is fresh. He remains at the top of the stairs, following Corky with his eyes like a poised hunter that has just spotted a target. He takes a half-step forward. His shoulders glide back, and his neck lengthens.

Corky cuts through the crowd with purpose. Behind him, Patty is turning his head so quickly from skirt to skirt that it looks like a loose bed knob. It seems inevitable that he will crash into a bowler's backswing or a

Ralph in 1949

table full of Coca-Cola bottles. As the two men stop, the volume of the venue seems to dial down in Ralph's head. Corky reaches out and gently grasps a soft, dainty hand. Patty is greeted with a white smile behind dark red lipstick, and by those deep hazel eyes.

They have found the girl Ralph was looking for.

A fantastic Saturday night draws to an end. Eva's party was a success, and she is getting ready to leave. Since Corky did not stay long, she swings her head around, looking for another friend with a car. That's when she catches a glimpse of Ralph bowling a few lanes over with a group of friends.

"Tootsie, oh crap! There's that Ralph guy that I stood up."

Ralph looks up instinctively.

"Darn it! He saw me!"

Ralph has avoided going over to talk with any of the models the whole evening. Now that their eyes have finally met, he begins to make his way over to Eva.

Eva grabs Tootsie and ducks into the bathroom. There they hide until it is nearly closing time.

Once they can't afford to wait any longer, the pair peek their heads out to find that all of their friends—and their rides—have left. They also see Ralph waiting at the bar.

"Oh, shit, don't tell me he's waiting for us!"

Tootsie and Eva slip out of the bathroom, hoping to leave unseen, but Ralph is there to greet them.

"Good evening, ladies. Do you need a ride?"

His offer is quickly refused.

Ralph takes Eva aside. "Look, I already told ya, I am a good guy," he whispers.

Billy Eckstine's "Blue Moon" has just begun to play over the sound system. It is one of Eva's favorite songs. Noticing that Eva's attention is piqued by the music, Ralph blurted, "Do you like this song? You wanna dance? I can dance real good."

Eva lets down her guard, in part because she feels silly for having hid so long. "All right."

They dance together in the middle of the bowling alley while the servers and late-shift crew clean up the venue. Their arms relax. Their touch feels more natural than it did a moment ago.

"Are you sure we've never met before?" Eva asks.

Ralph replies, "Yeah, you look familiar. Wait, you're a Clyde Matthews model, right? I remember you now. I was the guy that pretended to be a pattern maker for Evan-Picone. You know, at the factory in Jersey City."

"Oh, that was you?"

"Yeahhhh."

"Well, I thought you were a real son-of-a-bitch!"

"What?" Ralph lets loose a loud guffaw through a wide grin. "I guess I can be sometimes, but I didn't mean to be. Really, I just wanted to show Charles Evans that I could be a damn good pattern maker. I'm sick of sweeping floors. So I saw that they needed help and I just jumped in."

The tune concludes, and the Playdrome staff rushes the three young adults out of the bowling alley.

As they shuffle to Ralph's car so he can drive them home, Tootsie pulls Eva in close and whispers, "Oh my God, what the hell was that?"

Eva can't hide the pursed smile stuck on her lips.

Time passes, and now that she has graduated from Barbizon, Eva's career takes off. She knows that if she is to ever make it big, then she needs to think big. So she takes on more challenging gigs.

The hard-working model is well aware of the short lifespan afforded to most others in the industry. A modeling career usually only lasts from sixteen to nineteen years of age. If she is going to make the most of this short-lived career, then she needs to move onto a more adult-focused agency. For this reason, Eva chooses to say farewell to Clyde Matthews after only about a year.

Eva wants to model garments geared toward audiences over the age of sixteen and to move toward a mainstream career. She can envision herself as a household face, though not necessarily a household name. This is because she is unsure what name she will be using. All the stars have Jewish-sounding names, so "Eve Aris" finally turns into "Carol Chase." Delores Parker—known by her stage name "Tanya Weinstein"—is a bit short and stocky compared to other models, but she knows the industry and is a good friend. She encourages Eva to explore her career at Conover Modeling Agency. She shares the phone number of her only contact at Conover's.

Harry Conover, the lead agent and owner of Conover Modeling Agency, created "cover girls," a description that lives on in the modern day through the cosmetics line he licensed under that name. Now that Eva has been accepted at Conover, she is expected to do runway and wholesale work. The top model at Conover's is Candy Jones, who voluntarily serves as Eva's mentor, taking Eva under her wing. Candy gets Eva her first professional headshots at Dorick & Dorick, a Manhattan photography studio known for shooting stars of stage and screen.

Once she is fully settled in at Conover's, the booking agents waste no time sending Eva on go-sees and landing gigs. With only a limited resume, Eva lands her first of many magazine jobs. She is chosen to pose in a *Seventeen* magazine centerfold with about a dozen other girls. This magazine work is being done while Eva also continues as a runway model. She is on a roll, but Candy warns her against developing any ego. The wrong attitude will lose Eva unexpected opportunities. One such opportunity comes around in the form of a toothpaste advertisement that Eva feels downright silly posing in. But Eva shows up on time, works the camera as a professional model must, and literally grins and bears it.

Much to Eva's surprise, that advertisement makes it into *Glamour* magazine. What follows is her first cover shoot. *US Camera* presents Eva wearing a heavy, aviation-inspired leather jacket with a wool-lined collar, crouched in drizzling rain and modeling a professional camera.

These print gigs wax and wane, but coupled with runway, Eva is working consistently. Some shoots even pay more than five dollars an hour. She isn't making enough money, however, to regularly use buses or taxis,

U.S. Camera photoshoot

and she definitely cannot afford a car. As a result, her body takes a beating as she walks all over the city.

Despite her busy schedule, Eva spends more and more of her free time with Ralph. The pair run around Manhattan clubs, Brooklyn bars, and New Jersey lounges. They see every new band that shows up at the Paramount Theatre in Times Square. They drink whiskey with the Irish along St. John's Place, and Eva jitterbugs while Ralph networks the bar at Frank Daily's Meadowbrook Ballroom in suburban Cedar Grove.

They love the bar and club scene, especially Ralph, who has big plans of his own to start a club called Club Domino. Both Ralph's father and his youngest brother are named Dominic, both of whom Ralph cares for deeply. Ralph dedicates himself to learning everything he can about the service industry and the business of evening entertainment. Together, he and Eva grow and grow.

CHAPTER 11

"THERE IS NO DISCOVERY WITHOUT RISK, AND WHAT YOU RISK REVEALS WHAT YOU VALUE." — JEANETTE WINTERSON, 'WRITTEN ON THE BODY'

Ralph's strong personality has always been apparent, but as his and Eva's relationship blossoms, he begins to dig his heels in. A bit of jealousy creeps to the surface. Ralph is frustrated by the male models, the ill-intentioned agents, and the photographers. The entertainment business brings negative attention in more ways than Ralph can count, and he has had enough of it. If Eva is to be his girl, he tells her, then she has to stop pursuing her modeling career.

Ralph makes this ultimatum not because Eva isn't trustworthy, but because men in positions of power tend to get what they want, regardless of what the talent has to say about it. This is especially true for performers with a real shot at a career. Without influential people working in their favor, a performer can never be in the position to showcase their talent. As with the Macy's man on the day Ralph and Eva first met, these opportunities often come with unwanted strings attached.

Eva has made herself a target. With Ralph insistent upon her removing that target, she now has to decide what she wants most in life.

Eva cares for Ralph and does not want him to think she is a run-around. In addition to that, she likes strong men. Her beauty and her will usually intimidate the men she dates, but not Ralph. Eva does feel that he is being overprotective, but Ralph knows what he wants and is not about to compromise.

He is twenty-five, seven years older than Eva. He is a traditional Italian man, and he is looking forward to a life building his own family. He never needed a model. He needs his Eve.

In the heat of a budding relationship, Eva follows her heart. She is giving up the chance of a lifetime... but perhaps it is somebody else's chance, somebody else's opportunity, somebody else's dream now. She has experienced success she is proud of, but she, too, wants a family of her own. She wants to marry the love of her life, her soulmate, and she has found him. She is more than her photos to Ralph. She is more than the clothes she displays for *Seventeen* or on the runway. She is more than the smile she learned to flash at Barbizon.

Models usually have a three-year career. This moment in time, captured by a camera and splashed on the pages of a magazine, means eternal life, but it is also haunted by the impending end to an exciting adventure for all but the most exceptional. Is Eva one of those few "exceptional" who can travel the world for the rest of their lives, living off the prestige of their smiles and frames?

Maybe. But probably not.

Eva isn't done. She has more to do, to give, to experience, and to create. But she walks, this time, away from modeling.

On April 21 of 1949, at the age of nineteen, adorned head-to-toe in white satin, Eva recites her vows in front of family and friends. She weds an exuberant but steady Ralph Grimaldi. Together, just as Antonia and Gustavo had done in a rural region of Italy some years before, they become a new family: the Grimaldis.

Wedding of Ralph Grimaldi and Eva Ovarsi, April 1949

Gustavo walking Eva down the aisle

Wedding of Ralph Grimaldi and Eva Ovarsi, April 1949

Left to right: Eva and Gustavo, [background] Ralph

Ralph has been saving money, and soon after their marriage begins, he approaches his wife seeking something he has never sought before: her help.

"Evie, let's open the bar. Bob and I got it all figured out, but I need you to round up the girls, get the word out." Bob Calleja, a cousin of Ralph's, is a partner lined up to manage shifts.

"Look, there are bars everywhere. What are you going to do?" Eva probes.

"The markup on liquor is huge. We don't need to be greedy. We'll undercut everybody and charge at the door to see acts. You could even sing if you wanted to! We'll be the best place for new music."

With a clear strategy in place, the couple purchase the Blue Flame on Kennedy Boulevard and open Club Domino. It is the only venue selling shots of whiskey for fifty cents, with thirty-five cents for a shot of rye. The Club soon becomes an after-hours hotspot for the service industry employees who arrive in droves after their shifts end. Ralph advertises in the local papers, and musicians start coming in for on-mic jam sessions each weekend. Any musician can come and participate in any one of the club's three private rooms.

The drummer from Glenn Miller stops in regularly. Sylvia Reed, a pop singer with a growing following, is offered a taste of the cover charge to perform each week. Johnny Rio of The New York Trio, a popular local band, is another of Ralph's cousins, and he becomes a mainstay at the club. Johnny plays bass, John Galizzio plays guitar, and the singer, Casso, completes the trio. They are such a pull that Club Domino takes them in as partners. The new ownership changes the name of the bar to the Club New Yorker, and they become the most successful club in the area. Late nights pour over into packed afternoons, where impromptu acoustic performances erupt and patrons fill every seat and clamor for space with their friends on the floor. Ralph realizes they have found a winning formula that can be replicated.

Times are good. Eva and Ralph are having a blast. And life will soon get even better.

Later, in October of 1950, Eva gives birth to her first child. She is the first to have a grandchild on either side of the family, so she's very nervous. Saint Mary's Hospital, the same hospital Eva was brought to in order to get forged paperwork nearly two decades earlier, has a ten-bed nursing ward run entirely by nuns. While a bit delirious from interspersed contractions, Eva can hear a band playing outside in the park across the street. It is Columbus Day, and Garden Street is swarming with people. At 12:15 p.m., Eva's first child is born, and the attending nun names her "Christine." Eva feels it is a good Catholic name and that the girl will lead a good life.

But when the nun hands Christine to her, Eva notices that something is not quite right with the child's eyes. On closer inspection, the baby girl is actually a boy... and Asian!

"This is not my baby!" screams the new mother.

By no coincidence, the Asian woman in the bed next to Eva is nursing a baby girl. The nun plucks Christine off the other woman's breast and hands her back to Eva.

A few days later, Iona, who is pregnant herself, helps Eva home. Ralph has prepared the home with a beautiful bassinet and has laid out pink clothes for Christine's first days out of the hospital. Eva doesn't even feel comfortable changing the infant's clothes, she's so nervous. But *Dr. Spock's Baby and Child Care* gives Eva the early directions and the confidence to assume the role of a new mother. It instructs her on how to sterilize everything, how to bathe and swaddle the baby, and how to burp and comfort her little one.

Beautiful baby Christine, with her thick black hair... in fact, does look a little Asian, thinks Eva.

Life continues to move swiftly for the couple. One after another after another, Ralph and Eva's clubs begin sprouting up all around New Jersey. They are now running The Club New Yorker, The Happy Hour, The Apartment Lounge, The Hole in the Wall, and Club 13, all at the same time. Although Eva never officially works in the clubs, she is an owner by virtue of being Ralph's wife, and that keeps her very busy. She helps clean, inspects and accepts deliveries, does inventory for the clubs, and addresses the accountant. She also pursues an associate's degree at Drake College of Business—prodded, as always, by Iona—while Ralph continues working in textiles at Evan-Picone during the day, eventually becoming the pattern maker he always promised he'd be. At night, he manages the clubs alongside his beloved wife Eva. The two feel as if there is no limit to how much they can grow.

The Grimaldis also have a fantastic relationship with all of their guests. Ralph bets huge, brawny men that his petite Evie can best them in arm-wrestling matches. With a laugh and a swig, they each slap a dollar bill on the table and take a seat across from Ralph's wife. After they clasp hands and prepare for battle, a smile curls on Eva's lips as she slides her foot up the inner thigh of her competitor. The spectators howl as Eva conquers one unsuspecting brute after another.

Three years later, the clubs are still thriving. While Eva prepares to open each day, she brings little Christine along. One afternoon at Club New Yorker, Christine climbs up the stage and grabs a loose microphone off the floor..

"I'm a little teapot, short and stout..." sings Christine.

Eva is thrilled there is another singer in the family. "Ohhh, yayyyyyy!" The proud mother applauds. "What else can you sing?"

Christine begins to belt the lyrics of "Jesus, Jesus, Come to Me."

Smiling, Eva slips into daydream about her life as a performer. She misses the drama and glam, but she has traded that for something much greater: the adventure, excitement, and satisfaction of raising her family.

"To my Ralph, All my love, All my life. Your Evie 12/5/49"

My Dearest Family,

My hope is that with this letter I can impart upon you some lessons I have learned from my past experiences, and perhaps those lessons will help you live wonderful, fulfilling, and happy lives long after I am no longer here to comfort you during a time of need.

The many stories of my youth may seem glamorous, but if you've listened carefully you would understand that life was hard. I was alone and, believe it or not, I was scared. But growing up in an immigrant family, I knew no one was going to make my dreams come true but me. I was lucky enough to have a supportive family, but beyond a few well-timed words of encouragement, there was nothing more they could do. I had to figure out my own path. Although uneducated and naïve, I was strong in many other ways. My independence forced me to encounter many trials, some ending in error and others in success, but the lessons I learned were enough for me to raise myself throughout life and into a great-grandmother. Since you are all living through more prosperous times than we were and have the support of family, there is no reason why you cannot achieve your dreams while avoiding life's many pitfalls.

Don't just "follow" your dreams. Take an active role to grab hold of them. No one is going to make your dreams come true for you--at least not for a price. Work hard, get educated, and take personal responsibility for achieving greatness. The burden is ultimately on you to do what's necessary to achieve your dreams.

Be a good person. Fame and fortune obtained by harming others or yourself will never amount to success. The toll such a life takes on you is not worth any material gains it might bring. Just as Ralph and I are the foundation for our family—each generation more educated and more successful than the one before it—you must be that foundation for your children and your children's children. To do that, you'll have be a role model for multiple generations of loved ones.

Listen to me, never forget what I am telling you now. I will not be here forever but I will always be looking down on you and you can always ask for my help. I will hear you, and let that place you at ease when you are struggling to figure out the next step in your life.

Keep my memory in your heart. Treat your children like they are the only children in the world. Love them and guide them and never hurt them in any way. I don't just love you, I live for you, and I would give my life for you.

All My Love,

Grandma
(2014)

AFTERWORD

"THERE IS A FOUNTAIN OF YOUTH: IT IS YOUR MIND, YOUR
TALENTS, THE CREATIVITY YOU BRING TO YOUR LIFE AND
THE LIVES OF THE PEOPLE YOU LOVE."
— SOPHIA LOREN

After the events of this story, Eva stayed active and social by engaging
in local and state politics. She was voted into the Palisade's Park Women's
Republican Club as Club President. This particular branch was very active
and known for its effective fundraisers. The Women's Republican Club
worked alongside the Men's Republican Club to fund their favored
campaigns for elective office. The most common way of fundraising was by
selling small items such as socks, stockings, and men's neckties.

Eva's inner knowledge of the nightclub and entertainment business gave
her another idea: card games. She began throwing card parties, where
money would be donated to the Club while people had a fun night rubbing
elbows with the local politico. These card parties grew into countywide
events. If you were running for office, attending a card party was more
effective than any town hall speech or Q&A session.

Eva took particular interest in throwing card parties for the Hackensack
judgeship election. Andrew Napolitano was an accomplished attorney and
something of a local celebrity. The suburbs were swelling with the aging
wave of Italian immigrants that began their lives in the shadows of New
York skyscrapers, and Andrew shared their heritage and their conservative
ideals. He was a kind and charismatic man. After a very successful night of
card games—which led to him becoming Judge Napolitano—he personally
thanked Eva and made a promise that if she ever needed a favor in the

future, he would oblige in any way he could.

Iona was married to a man named Joel Edison in the same year Eva married Ralph: in fact, she was married first, as the oldest sister, followed by Eva in April, and then their sister Linda later in the same year, each wedding proceeding by age. Iona went to college immediately after graduating high school, first attending New Jersey City University, then St. Peter's University. She eventually moved out of state, raised her own family, and passed away in 2014 after a long and happy life.

Antonia's death in 1970 was caused by liver problems stemming from alcoholism, which plagued her after the death of her son Mario. Her husband Gus lived in a senior living home after her passing, and eventually was taken care of by his daughters Linda and Eva as his age advanced. He passed away in 1990, after ninety-three years, two world wars, and the births of many, many loving children and grandchildren.

After raising four children of their own, Eva and Ralph moved to Toms River, New Jersey, in 1980. Eva was the oldest person on the block, a far cry from the days when she was clubbing or even running fundraisers. Ralph passed away in 2000 at the age of seventy-six. Eva's neighborhood today is full of trusted friends, and the children, in particular, take good care of her. She feels blessed to have the love and support of so many.

ENDNOTES

1. Ancestry.com. (2007). "Passenger Ships and Images." Retrieved from http://search.ancestry.com/cgi-bin/sse.dll?db=passengerships&h=92&ti=0&indiv=try&gss=pt

2. Oh, Ranger!. (n.d.). "The Immigrant Journey." Retrieved from http://www.ohranger.com/ellis-island/immigration-jounrey

3. Shaw, D. V. (1994). *Immigration and ethnicity in New Jersey history.* Trenton: New Jersey Historical Commission, Dept. of State.

4. Hoboken411. (2010, January 28). "Some Hoboken History about The Fabian Theater and Shop Rite at Newark and Washington Streets." Retrieved from https://hoboken411.com/archives/36466

All other information was taken from interviews with Eva Grimaldi.

PICTURE CREDITS

Page
3:	Public domain
15:	Family photo
24:	Hoboken Historical Museum
29:	Family photo
37:	Hoboken Historical Museum
44:	Family photo
47:	Hoboken Historical Museum
52:	Family photo
60:	Family photo
64:	Family photo
68:	Family photo
69:	Family photo
73:	Family photo

ABOUT THE AUTHOR

Anthony W. LoCascio is an attorney who works with pharmaceutical and healthcare industry clients in the Greater New York metropolitan area. He has enjoyed writing all his life, but it was his legal education that sparked an interest in nonfiction and historical themes. His only prospective audience for *A Message From Overseas* was, originally, his grandmother Eva, but after digging into the substance of the story, he felt there are others who would benefit from reading about the subject's journey.

Made in the USA
Middletown, DE
04 June 2019